Growing Up Cowboy

Growing Up Cowboy

Confessions of a Luna Kid

A personal chronicle by
Ralph Reynolds

Fulcrum Publishing
Golden, Colorado

Cover design by Jody Chapel, Cover to Cover Design
Cover illustration by William Marlow

Two chapters in this book were published previously in approximately the same form. "Luna Kid Comes Out" appeared in *Persim-
mon Hill*, vol. 14, no. 3 (1984). "Let a Dead Horse Rest" appeared in
Do You Remember Luna . . . 100 Years of Pioneer History, 1983.

Library of Congress Cataloging-in-Publication Data

Reynolds, Ralph, 1930–
        Growing up cowboy : confessions of a Luna Kid /
        Ralph Reynolds.
             p.   cm.
        ISBN 1-55591-086-6 (pbk.)
        1. Reynolds, Ralph, 1930– —Childhood and youth.
     2. Cowboys—New Mexico—Biography. 3. New Mexico—
     Biography. 4. New Mexico—Social life and customs.
     5. Ranch life—New Mexico. I. Title.
     F801.R48A3   1991
     .978.9'05'092—dc20   91-71366
     [B]   CIP

Printed in the United States of America

0   9   8   7   6   5   4   3   2   1

Fulcrum Publishing
350 Indiana Street
Golden, Colorado 80401

To Mother

Ever a Shining Lady,
she glitters at age ninety-nine

Contents

Prologue

B ecause our past looms over us always, some part of what most authors write can be called autobiographical. However, the stories of the Luna Kid that follow are 100% pure autobiography. Each adventure, incident, conversation—even the thoughts, dreams, fears that spring in and out of the Kid's mind—are recollections from my boyhood.

I've written those experiences in present tense and third person because tense and person don't impinge on facts or truth, but they can diminish reading ease and enjoyment.

Present tense I've borrowed from the art and style of the storyteller and jokester. Why do they so often tell their tales in present tense? To get and hold attention, of course. Hearing a story as it seems to be happening bridges gaps in time, sort of puts listeners and readers on-scene with the action.

I don't know why I wrote this in third person, probably because I wanted to. That's not an acceptable rationale, of course. So let's just say that a lighthearted, sometimes self-effacing autobiography seems to work better if there are not a lot of I's and we's interspersed through it. Besides, we wouldn't want the author to sound like a masochist. And there's something else. After prowling through all those skeletons in his closet, I'm not altogether proud of the sometimes loutish Luna Kid. What better way to wash my hands of him than to cast him forever in third person?

Ralph Reynolds
alias Luna Kid

Growing Up Cowboy

Luna Kid
Comes Out

He can feel tension within the arena, heightened by an expectant hush all around. His ride has been announced with a strained, almost funereal formality. Now they are waiting, watching, hardly breathing. He is quite sure of that.

The Kid's body stiffens into a posture of carefree defiance. He looks down across the shining back of his adversary. The bull commences to tremble. He wishes it wouldn't do that because now a tremor is starting in the knee that holds the Kid braced against one side of the pen. Hell's afire! Would they please hurry before somebody notices, but not hurry too fast. This bull has never been rode, and they both are trembling. But now the arena is quiet, and he is ready. He wants to say "hurry up with the damned surcingle," but he knows if he tries it that his teeth will chatter and he will stammer on the "surc-" part.

Now they have the rope around the bull, and Kid reaches down his free hand. His knuckles touch the bull,

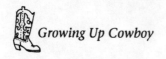

and he feels the taut energy of the beast at the back of his fingers. His fist closes powerfully around the rope, and he draws it up tight against his palm. Now his fingers clamp against the loose end of the surcingle, and he knows his time has come. He swings a levi-clad leg out across the haunches of the bull and settles slowly down to straddle it, catching his breath at the sensation of hairy primordial warmth along the length of his thighs. The arena is even quieter now. Quieter than death. They know what is to come. Will the audience be trembling, too?

"You ready?" someone asks.

"Not yet." It burst out too quickly. He must take care not to sound scared when he isn't.

He looks down at the thrust-out face below, with its dripping nostrils and rolling eyes. The bull is trembling again now. He can smell the heavy, rich, rumenized breath of the animal wafting up around his own nostrils, and he repeats, "Not yet," as he clasps and unclasps his hand on the surcingle.

They'll be ready now and waiting. No man has ever seen this rider thrown or this bull rode. They want blood, do they? He'll show 'em blood. Anger flashes down his neck and arm, tightening his hold on the surcingle. The bloodthirsty devils are gonna get what they want. The fear that had come with the night, lying there alone in the dark, and again with the morning, peering through the poles at the bull, vanishes against his fist, so tightly clenched on that surcingle. And he hollers, "Let 'im go."

The acceleration strikes against his clinging hand like a heavy weight at the rope's end. Then a jarring stop throws his head out in front of his shoulders. He rolls forward, heels skidding toward the bull's flanks, and feels the sudden sharp pain of a testicle caught between his own flanks and the spine of the bull. Lord! How it hurts. And then the bull is bucking in angry, darting, spastic moves and emitting mad and murderous bellows. For an instant he is hanging there, touching the bull only with his hand, finally throwing himself forward just in time for his crotch to wedge against a shoulder of the bull. He is losing his straddle, slipping too far to the left, feeling himself falling, his legs up and out as they go by a post. It slaps against his right shin, knocking him upright again, saving the fall.

Now he can hear the yelling and cheering, but it is too late. His grip has broken. He is falling forward, both hands on the bull's neck and then the slippery ears. Bull slobber is mixing with his own and wetting his face. He is flipping helplessly over the head and under the chest of the bull. His face is sliding across the ground, and then his head strikes something hard. He feels the bull go over his prone body, hooves slashing across his face and onto his throat, hammering hard against his groin.

He lies there, semi-stunned. There is pain like a fire in his leg. He can taste blood and manure, and one eye is packed with it. He is dizzy. His groin feels as if it has been shot away from his body. And then he hears the swelling chorus of shouts.

He painfully draws his knees under him and grabs a rail of the fence, pulling himself up to a standing position. He stoops there, blinking. At last he can see people. They are whooping and hollering. Over by the gate, the Hereford calf contentedly reaches through the slats to nibble a blade of grass. The surcingle still hangs loose around its body. A compact, dangling scrotum attests to masculinity.

The Kid licks his dry lips. Fresh manure spills onto his tongue and seeps in through his open mouth. A shadow flits across the patty-littered floor of the crude aspen-pole corral. He looks up. Three chicken hawks wheel with curiosity there above the trees, sole witnesses along with his brothers to the coming out of a rural cowboy.

I Was a
Concave Cowboy

G iven that a home of hand-hewn logs is properly called a cabin, it can be stated without license that the Luna Kid was conceived, gestated, birthed, weaned, reared, and matriculated into the world from a log cabin astride the 34th parallel, in the unincorporated Valley of Luna, State of New Mexico, his birth having been recorded in the annals of Catron County, year of the mule, 1930.

Born to an economically distressed land and the likewise stressed household of a peasant rancher, mothered by a bright, loving and competent, but undersized and much overworked granddaughter of a polygamist, and godfathered only by the Great Depression, the Luna Kid nevertheless persevered, even finally mastering enough of the English language to record and elaborate the events herein. (This chronicle makes no presumption to literature, high or low, although its objective is perhaps an immodest one: to add a small, but definitive footnote to the voluminous legend of the cowboy. One might call it

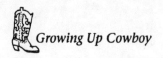

perspective.) Though having been born into an under-privileged family of seven, the Luna Kid showed, as judged by rare photos of him, few ravages of deprivation. But photos can tell half-truths, as we shall see.

The mouth appeared ever tightly closed and arrow straight, and in the early years, the hair never combed. Deceptively shy and bright-seeming eyes slanted downward toward the earlobes, as did eyes in photos of his Irish ancestors (even though those same Celts provided less than half his pedigree). That he proved to be nothing special as a student, except in a negative sense, could perhaps be laid either to an ordinary aptitude or to lack of correction for those same eyes, which turned out to be severely near-sighted and astigmatic. (He used to sneak out his mother's old spectacles to take to the movies.) In any case, when he finally did receive glasses of his own at about age twelve, they failed to raise his grades in school.

The Kid proved shy only in appearance. He read constantly and was inclined to talk a lot, often butting-in and attempting to dominate conversations. Like most people who talk too much and read a lot, he used and misused many big words, to the entertainment (and sometimes amusement) of chums and townsfolk.

As we have seen and shall see again, the Kid was not lavishly endowed with bravery or brawn. However, he proved muscular and mobile enough to become a fair athlete, except for an abysmal lack of cool in team sports. He achieved champion status in chinning and broad jump. But in football, though he tackled like a tiger, he never knew where the pigskin was. He could leap high and block shots of opposing basketball players, but his team-mates never passed to him, for they quickly learned that Kid hated the notoriety and insecurity of having the ball. He'd drop the thing or toss it away to anybody, including the other team, just to be rid of it. A surreptitious, though good-natured chant at County High went: "Lunatic, Lunatic, he's our man. If he can't lose it, nobody can."

Kid might likewise have proven attractive to girls, his face being relatively "clean cut," as they said in those days, except that he seldom smiled, especially around girls, for to do so would expose front teeth deeply etched with black holes. Indeed, one tooth decayed so badly that when Kid was eighteen, Army dentists summarily pulled it, thereby avoiding the trouble and expense of filling such a cavity. (An expedient cop-out considering the military would provide neither bridges nor crowns. They apparently thought it preferable for a G.I. to be seen by the public with a hole in his mouth rather than a hole in his tooth.)

In dress, the oldest photo of the Luna Kid now extant, a class portrait from about the fourth grade, has him decked out in detested bib overalls. Shortly thereafter, however, roughly simultaneous with his coming out, he advanced into the much coveted rural cowboy garb of unsanforized levis, an open-collar shirt, and brogans. (Kids from smaller families got to wear boots with underslung heels in place of brogans.) Until he entered the military, the Kid was seldom seen in anything else except when he graduated from high school wearing, in addition, the necktie that had adorned three older brothers at graduation. This had nothing to do with tradition or sentimentality. It was simply the only tie in the house.

If this apparel seems dreary, the reader must remember that the laws of permutation apply even to simple rural cowboy duds. Thus, combinations are limited only by the quantities of individual items. The Kid generally was supplied with three pairs of levis a year, obtained at intervals of about four months. So at any given time, he could count on having one pair, fully shrunk, slightly faded, and freshly washed, for dress-up. A second pair, well faded and preferably slightly soiled, was for school.

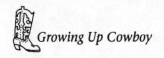

The third pair, being faded to grey, fully soiled, frayed and patched, and comfortably stretched, was perfect for chores and work. Because cowboys don't wear out shirts, a good selection was always available, mostly community property or hand-me-downs, and mostly of flannel or light denim. But Kid's mother always saw to it that he had a clean white one of his own.

* * * * *

Come dress-up time, the Kid draws from the well a round washtub of water and heats it atop the kitchen stove for a bath. He polishes the brogans, pulls on the clean-smelling bluest levis, with wrinkles there where Mother's flat iron has butted against the rivets. He puts on the white shirt, leaving the top two buttons undone, and neatly rolls both sleeves up almost to the shoulders. Then he stuffs a blue bandana into the taut, left, hind pocket of the levis. (If the pants fit properly, there's no way you can get a hand in there.) He tugs one corner of the hankie out a ways so it hangs down just enough to cover about half his pocket. Finally, when nobody will notice, he slips past the huge old ornate cookstove in the kitchen to snatch a quick look at his reflection. A cowboy blossoms there in the shiny concave trim as youthful shoulders broaden and waist narrows—a truly heroic image.

"Pretty snupersent." Kid's mother smiles her pride and approval.

The Luna Kid is dressed up and ready to go. Anywhere.

A Country This Sorry
Has to Be Prime

L una Valley, even today, is the essence of cowboy land. Indeed, the birthplace of the Luna Kid lies only a stone's throw or two from the headwaters of the Blue River, birthplace of that most famous (or infamous) of all one-named Americans: Geronimo, himself a notorious cowboy as well as cow thief, etc.—that "etcetera" glossing over a lot of unsavory territory.

In our time, grazing of cattle is considered lowest among the many potential agricultural uses of land. It follows, then, that people would put to grazing only that land unsuited for other use. Carrying this thought a little further, it is easy to establish that the rough and tumble Mogollon Breaks lying on either side of the New Mexico–Arizona border is country so poor that it has to be the prime cowboy land of the earth.

Conceived in the fire and brimstone of Tertiary volcanos, this wild, wooded cowboy country, ever mysterious, sometimes graceful to the eye and sometimes awe-

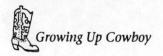

some, is also almost useless to man. For where it is warm enough to grow his crops, it is too dry. And where it is moist enough for crops, it is too cold. And even if we could magically change the climate of this land, to warm the heights and moisten the steppe, it is everywhere too rough and rocky except for the toughest of cowboys and the ruggedest of cows.

This land is also vastly underpopulated, thanks mainly, perhaps, to the aforementioned native son, Geronimo, and his ilk. Generations of pioneers were stalled from settling there, for the mountains and the valleys had long before been chosen by Apache warriors as their own. Even the Spanish kings seem to have had no enemies hated or feared enough to deserve banishment into such useless and dangerous territory. Thus, the region was never included in any of the many royal land grants that gave away much of New Mexico.

In the end, the beneficiary of all this was the United States public domain, which at the turn of the century, claimed the vast unsettled province as national forest land. This has preserved the Gila, Blue, and White Mountain wildernesses, unspoiled and largely untapped even today. Untapped, that is, by all except the cowboy and his cows.

In modern times, as we're so often sloganized, the mountain cowboy lands of the West have been invaded by other "multiple" uses, including various kinds of recreation, especially skiing, plus mining, lumbering, and so on. As we shall see, the Luna cowboys indeed encountered, or confronted, some of these uses, but in the main their land has proven too dry for fishing, too low for skiing, too high for health spas, too lonely and primitive for general recreation, and too remote for mining.

Their land was cowboy land, and it remains so. Yet, the cowboy land of the Mogollon Breaks, its climate governed by undulating altitudes and its terrain by fits and starts and faults within the native rocks, was and remains as variable from suburb to center as is any large city of the earth.

The stompin' grounds of the Luna Kid were somewhat higher in elevation than the mean of this land. And due partly to the erosive forces of gathering waters, the higher ground of the Mogollon Breaks has remained less wrinkled and rough than the lower. In fact, some of the high terrain, though horribly rocky, is level as a prairie, having been laid down by runny sheets of lava that poured out over ancient wetlands. The resulting flats are strewn with agate, bordered by cliffs, and drained by many shallow draws and a few deep canyons.

Even the intrepid Zane Grey, who finally nested on the Mogollon Rim, never wrote of the border Breaks, having been mesmerized by those nice and lovely crimson canyons on to the west of there. The region was one time lightly touched, though, by a pen less popular but more majestic than Grey's.

Early in the century, Aldo Leopold rode out over the same high rustic flats and seams that the Kid was born to, scouting timber for a young Forest Service. Years later, in his monumental *Sand County Almanac*, the naturalist remembered his experience rather incidentally but with unerring sensual flair. He described the land of the Kid as: "a confusion of wooded mesas. Each hollow seemed its own small world, soaked in sun, fragrant with juniper, and cozy with the chatter of piñon jays, but top out on a ridge and you at once became a speck in an immensity. . . . "

Sometimes there wasn't a penny in the log cabin called home, but the Luna Kid was born to no poverty.

4

Pity No Critter
That Kicks

It is important for the reader to realize that, as with most occupations, ordinary activities of a rural cowboy include some tasks that are not glamorous or even attractive and a few that are quite grubby. The reader will therefore be in a correct frame of mind for the confessions that follow.

Nowadays in the corn belt of Iowa or Illinois, one occasionally hears or reads in local farm magazines of suspected ritualistic slashings of farm animals. The poor creatures have become apparent victims of unspeakable atrocities, committed by unknown cultists, nihilistic pranksters, or even visitors from outer space. Such orgies in animal-hate, if that's what they are (some say it's merely the work of roving dogs), may seem frightful to fat-stock farmers and pet lovers. But they appear relatively tame, in a way even merciful, when compared with the mutilations at one time observed, and sometimes perpetrated with gusto, by the Luna Kid.

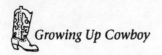

The time has come to speak of branding calves. But before we proceed, it seems useful to lay to rest any notions regarding the innocence of the victim. Please bear in mind that before the rural cowboy approaches a bound and helpless calf with his diabolical instruments, the cowboy has likely been dragged, butted, bitten, slobbered on, crapped on, and perversely and roundly kicked in several tender areas. In fact, in his advanced years, Daddy, a legendary rider of wild broncs, suffered such a calf-kick to the inside of his right knee that a broken ligament hobbled him for life.

Let us shed no tears, then, for the writhing little beast who becomes the brandee and much more in this strenuous and rather messy encounter. After all, the poor animal suffers it and displays no great resentment afterwards. Maybe this indicates an innate stupidity on his part, or perhaps it's just that he has plenty of reason to feel grateful that it's over and happy that he's still alive.

* * * * *

The Luna Kid would enjoy the roundup at branding time. It's warm and damp now in rainy season, and the air is brightly clean, washed of its dust. The pines smell good. The grass, weeds, bushes, and flowers, bursting and swollen with sudden frantic growth, seem brighter in color and twice their usual size. Cattle are scattered this time of year—so the Kid gets to go off alone.

It's grand to be horseback and alone in the bright morning. He kicks Bludog into a trot across Trout Creek and up the trail to the broad ridge between Snider Place and Steele Flat. Daddy said the Kid would find Redgut and her calf by the state-line fence. He is to drive her back toward the Steele Flat, picking up any other cows along the way. There may be some lone yearlin's up there. If so, leave 'em be. Watch specially for that brindle cow they'd bought from Uncle Dorf last fall. She might have lost her calf. The muley cow with the tore ear was likely up on the ridge, too. She had an early calf, and it better sure get branded now, or it'd be a chore to wrestle down later.

The Kid trots on alone. He picks up the brindle cow first and pushes her along, but she doesn't want to go. She slows to a walk and bawls. A calf answers and pops out of the brush, a dandy little whiteface bull, lively and hungry. He stops the brindle to suck, impatiently butting her teats, demanding. The Kid yells, "Git on. Git on." He rides up close and whacks the calf with the knot on the end of his rope. Bludog grabs with his teeth for the tailhead of the cow. She bursts away in a trot, the calf running backward, still trying to suck. Kid yells again, and Bludog is already in a high trot.

It's grand, really grand, to be a cowboy and alone in the woods, punching a wild cow off through the brush, yelling and spurring. If only Dia Felt could see him this minute.

He goes on a ways and picks up Redgut with her calf. The calf doesn't want to drive. It takes off back toward Trout Creek. Bludog whirls after it, hitting a bouncy sprint, the Kid holding on, feeling wind under his hat, ducking low branches of ponderosa. They turn Redgut's calf, and it dashes back toward its mother. Bludog pounds to a stop, throwing the Kid's thighs up against the swells of Lamar's saddle. He yells again at the calf, mostly in exuberance now.

That's cowboyin', and the Kid wishes it would go on and on. But at the Steele Flat he meets Dave, who's driven in from Underwood Mesa. They hear bawling and see Daddy has a bunch coming through the slot from Commor Draw.

They've got forty-five or fifty cows now. Some are Mcfate's. The herd moves compactly down Trout Creek toward the ranch. Dave and the Kid drive them around the

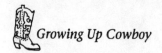

fence to the corral because there're oats planted in the fields. The cattle foolishly crowd through the gap in the corral, nervous and bawling, once inside pressing back against the poles and rolling their eyes. The older cows may remember what's ahead, having suffered it once and witnessed it six or eight times.

Pitch pine starts quick and hot, with smoke the blackness of malpais rock. The fire is big because it takes plenty of hot coals for the running irons, which are made from pokers or thick steel rods bent into a J.

Daddy lays out his instruments on a flat rock near the fire. There'll be hell to pay if the boys let a calf run across that rock. From a soiled canvas bag, he draws out a stubby pair of dehorners. Old Faundeer's calf was late last year and didn't get dehorned. Might need the nippers. Next, there's an oily box about ten inches long. It has the vaccinating needle and some vials of blackleg serum. Then there's a black pint Mason jar with a lid. Daddy finds a stick and ties a strip of bandana around it. He drops the cloth end into the stinking concoction called kersilic. Then he opens his Barlow pocket knife and lays that out. The irons are hot, and the rural surgeon, who doesn't know an antiseptic from an anesthetic and can't spell either, is ready. Bring on the calves.

There's more than one way to catch a calf. If it is big, approaching yearling, the best roper will catch both hind legs in a loop thrown from horseback. Then he will stretch out the calf 'til its body is suspended between its front legs and the tight rope. One strong cowboy merely grabs the calf's tail and pulls him over onto his back. Others grapple the lethal hooves and quickly tie all four legs together.

For a little smaller calf, a roper lassos the head from horseback. A flanker then follows the tight rope down to the calf and throws the wildly kicking little fellow by grabbing his neck in the left hand, his opposite rear flank in the right, and rolling him down one knee to the ground. Sounds systematic, but it's about as easy as lifting a Kawasaki upside down while the motor runs and the wheels spin.

This year's calves are small enough to rope and hold from on foot. But that makes the flanking even tougher because the roper sometimes gets dragged about before he can take a good half hitch around a post.

Max is doing the roping. He shakes out a stiff loop and stalks a calf. Makes no difference, now, which one. Cows glare at him, sometimes lowering their horns, and calves run behind their mothers. Each time he approaches a bunch, they split apart. He throws two loops that miss. The cattle are starting to run around the fence now. If he misses again, Daddy will make him give up the rope to Lamar.

Then the noose settles around the head of Redgut's little bull. Max braces the rope around his hips and drags the bucking calf out of the herd, excitedly demanding help. Kid rushes in. They fight the rope over to a post, and Max loops it for mechanical advantage, still holding the end to allow slack in case the calf chokes. Lamar and Dave ease down the rope to the calf. He's a tough one, bellowing and leaping. The dust boils up. Dave gets his handholds and lifts. Nothing doing. Calf won't budge. He's choking now, tongue hanging out one side of his mouth. Max gives some rope. Dave tries again. Calf gets a breath and charges right out of his grasp.

Kid looks around and notices that Daddy is grinning. Dave is swearing at the calf. He's limping from a hoof against his ankle. The corral is filling with dust and smoke, and there's a frantic chorus of bawling and mooing. Daddy is yelling instructions in his piercing voice. Dave has a better hold now. Calf jumps. Dave pulls up strong against the flank. Calf goes crashing down on his side with

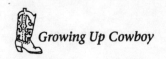

a bellow. He's trying to get up. Dave is grabbing for a front leg, has it. Calf still struggling. "Git yur knee in his belly," yells Daddy. It's more command than instruction. Dave moves his knee across calf's back and drops his weight there. He's ahold of the front leg. Calf is pinned.

Daddy walks in with a peggin' string, puts his shin up against the rear legs, and grabs the front ones. He loops the leather thong and draws it tight as Max gives rope to loosen the choke at the neck. They stand back, panting. The calf bawls and struggles. His mother runs up to check him with her nose. They shoo her away. The Kid checks the irons. That's his job. They're hot.

Daddy kneels at the back of the calf. "Hand me the knife." The calf's sides are heaving, his eyes rolling in terror. Daddy grabs the scrotum, stretching it out away from the testes, and whacks off its end with a single thrust of the knife. He pushes against the calf's stomach and white testicles pop out the cut end. He grabs one. The calf's stomach convulses. He scrapes off the cord attaching it. There's almost no blood. The other testicle has slipped back inside. He has to press the stomach again to bring it out. He scrapes it loose. A clean cut would cause bleeding. He hands both testicles to the Kid. "Lay 'em over on the fence. Fetch the kersilic."

The testicles are slick and firm. They feel like big warm beans. By the time the Kid lays them across the corral pole, they're sticky to the touch.

The calf lies there, neck stretched out. His eyes are rolled back but not glazed. The Kid is glad for him because that part is over. He dabs the open wound with kersilic. Calf doesn't show any pain now. Daddy grabs the left ear by the tip and stretches it. He cuts off two inches with a quick slash of the Barlow and tosses away the hairy triangular segment. A little blood bubbles out from the cut edge. Calf feels the knife, bellows and threshes, but again his eyes do not glaze. Daddy reaches around and grabs the left ear. The operation here is less deft, for he must cut a notch out of the lower part, deep enough to be noticeable even years from now. A brand is a legal mark, but it is the ear notch, varying between ranchers who share a range, that is most useful for quick identity. Daddy whacks out the notch, using none of the care displayed in castration. His hands are bloody now for the first time.

The Kid steps back, knowing and hating what comes next. Nothing doing, Daddy motions him over to the head of the calf. "Hold his nose." The Kid grabs the frothy nose and ducks his head just in time to miss the thin red stream that arches out to puddle on the dusty ground ten feet away. With about the same stroke you'd use to slice a carrot, Daddy's knife has whacked off a budding horn at the base. Calf is fighting against the Kid's hand, moving his head enough that the brothers, who've been standing near, have to dance about to avoid the bloody arch.

Daddy looks up to say something, but Dave, anticipating, is ready with a hot iron. He hands it to Daddy. There is a sizzle. Smoke boils up and the arch stops. The calf bawls, and its mother sticks her nose in close to the still-hot iron. In a moment, blood bubbles out again, and the iron touches down a second time. Sizzle and smoke, and the bubble stops. They turn the calf and duck again. A second stubby horn lies on the ground, and there's another bloody arch and sizzle and smoke again. The Kid carries over the syringe. Daddy lifts the skin of the front shoulder and sticks in the needle. The dumb calf indiscriminately bellows again.

Now the calf is on his right side, and Daddy reaches out a gloved hand to brush caked mud and manure off its rib cage. That's the signal. The Kid heads back to the fire for one of the pink-hot irons. This comes last because the brand has to stay clean. The Kid doesn't like the smell of

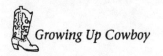

blue smoke rising from the burned hair and hide as Daddy prints out an eight-inch F and then a slightly larger Y next to it. What the Kid hates most, though, is the bellowing of the calf as Daddy goes back over the brand with a second hot iron.

Our new little steer lies there with heaving sides in the corral dust, which has been muddied here and there with his blood. His tongue is sticking out the left side of his mouth. His eyes are rolled back. His white hair reveals numerous bloody rivulets, and his red hair is wavy with sweat. In a few traumatic moments, his sex has been scraped away from his belly, and a significant portion of his ears has been removed. A part of his head has been cut away on each side and the resulting wounds scabbed with hot irons. He's been stuck with a needle, and his burned-in owner's I.D. stings across ten square-inches of his young hide, not to mention that the little fellow has been harshly choked, thrown down, and kneed in the neck and gut. But when that peggin' string is removed, stand back, because he's going to come off the ground like a stepped-on rattler. He runs bawling, heels kicking, and tail swinging to his mother. She licks at his bloody forehead and sniffs the scorched hair around his new brand.

By the time smoke from the next branding wafts across the corral, he's hungry and butting against his mother's teats as a signal to let him down some milk. His torture is over, but for the rural cowboys in the little corral, the bruising, dusty, bloody business at hand is just beginning. Hours later the corral floor is littered with pieces of ear and cut-off horns. It's over.

Miller Time never came to the old FY. But along toward the end of every branding day, Daddy would pick the firm little testicles off the fence and throw them rather carelessly into the dying coals of the branding fire. They would cook and swell and finally burst like marshmallows. The rural cowboys would fish them out of the coals with sticks and summarily, if wearily, eat them. Without beer.

Branding is an inescapable duty of a rural cowboy, right? Well, it ought to be, but the Luna Kid, in all his days as accessory to the fact, never branded a calf. He sometimes slashed the ears, whacked off horns, and even gingerly cauterized the bleeding wounds. But not once did he allow himself to touch that hot iron to the heaving sides of a little calf, or a big one. Not that the Kid was any kind of Caspar Milquetoast in his contacts with animals. Once he smashed twenty-eight lizards with stones in a grisly little contest with Sonny Boy who, losing, accounted only for twenty-two. Many times did he axe the heads off chickens without batting an eye, and one early morning he buried a stiff boot deep into the paunch of a gentle-eyed, old milk cow after she swished a crap-laden tail across his face. But even the Iron Kid had his limits, and in a cop-out so cunningly concealed that it would surprise his brothers even today, he never once branded a calf.

The Kid used to watch the brander apply that searing iron to the gentle side of a baby animal and wonder what the man himself felt. And gradually over time the realization came. Nothing. The Kid's Daddy and others of his age and persuasion felt nothing of the quivering anguish caused by their hot iron. But that kind of pain was transitory and to an end. Did they feel anything of animal pain? Ever?

* * * * *

One day the Kid and Daddy are driving toward Jenkins Creek to put out salt and gather a pickup load of wood. It is late in the high grazing season. All the cattle along the way are sleekly fat, until they come on a lone

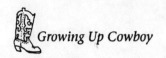

cow, barely standing, gaunt and drooped, about fifty yards to the left of the road. "Look at that," says Daddy.

"What's wrong with her?" asks the Kid, noticing a pastel-brown and wettish-looking streak along her curly white face.

"Looks like a horn's curved down and is growin' into her head," says Daddy. His shoulders move in something akin to a shudder. "That's a hell of a thing."

"Glad she ain't one of ours," says the Kid.

"It's Frank's cow," says Daddy. "Looks like she's lost her calf. Well, she's an old cow and no account."

He peers in silence and finally says, "Too bad we ain't got a horse."

They drive on, drop off the salt, and load up with a tangle of pine branches. On the way back, the cow stands there still. Daddy stops again and stares. Her head drops near her knees. Now and then a rear leg gives way, and her whole frail carcass jerks up to keep from falling over.

Finally Daddy says again, "I shore wished we had a horse." He sits peering at the cow and brooding. The Kid commences to fidget. He doesn't want to look at the old cow. His head aches just thinking about her. He is hungry and wants badly to get on home. After all, they'll have to unload the wood and do chores before supper.

"I got an idea," says Daddy. "There's a chute by the cabin at the Steele place. Son, go see if you can chase that old cow into the Steele Flat. I'll open the gate and help shoo her on into the chute."

The cow is weak with hunger and exhaustion but wild with pain. It takes more than an hour of chasing on foot to get her penned in the loading chute. The sun is going down by the time they get a close-up look at her ingrown horn. It has dipped down and penetrated maybe a half-inch into the skull just above the eye. It is aimed perfectly to grow right on through her brain. Blood and pus have blinded her eye, and a warm pink swelling distorts fully half her face.

"That's shore a fright," says Daddy. "There's a hacksaw in the tool box under the wood. You'll hafta unload to git at it while I tie her head down."

Unloading the wood, the Kid can hear noises of a fearsome struggle at the chute. There's thudding and crashing. The cow grunts and moans and once or twice emits a bellowing scream. If Daddy swears or raises his voice once, the Kid doesn't hear.

Slowly and carefully, the saw cuts into the horn, but each tiny vibration can be seen in the rolling pain-maddened eyes of the cow. Daddy is sawing as gently as a roughened rancher can saw. And he is talking supplications to an old cow who is so sick the Kid has to stand back in revulsion from the foul smells of her.

Afterwards they load the wood again and start home in the dusk. "I reckon that hole in her skull's gonna heal," says Daddy. "She'll git better."

"Yeah. Good," says the Kid.

"She sure perked up the minute we pulled that horn out of her head," says Daddy.

"Yeah," answers the Kid, thinking what it'll be like to do chores and again unload the tangled pile of wood, this time in the dark.

Daddy switches on the headlights of the pickup. "Too bad we'll be gittin' in so late," he says. He sounds almost apologetic, even though Daddy was never known to apologize for anything. The Kid nods.

"No need to unload the wood tonight," Daddy goes on. "That kin wait 'til mornin'. I'll do the milkin' when we git in."

The Kid has reason to be surprised, but somehow he isn't. He stretches with pleasure in the warm cab. He feels drowsy. His head doesn't ache anymore.

5

Sex on
the Range

I t has sometimes been noted that rural kids are preco-
cious in matters of sex. Seems that early in life they
have ample opportunity of associating the act of copula-
tion with reproduction; i.e., cow gets humped by bull, calf
results. At an early age, ranch kids have had opportunity
to observe sexual couplings typical of most species except
their own, and some have observed even that. Of course,
as they advance into puberty, they are already sophisti-
cated and relaxed in sexual matters. Therefore, rural
cowboys just naturally don't have so many unhealthy
hang-ups and appetites as their city-bred brethren.

That is somebody's hypothesis.

Another quite different notion is widely subscribed
to in literary or quasi-literary circles. This holds that rural
cowboys, due to isolation and deprivation, are engagingly
reticent and bashful regarding sex. It's a wisdom that has
come down to us in a thousand scenarios: the only act
more feared by a rural cowboy than making a sexual

25

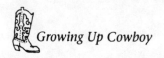

advance is receiving one. A related belief is that the rural cowboy is so gallant that he will take no woman except the one who must have him, and then only after he has won the right and privilege to do so. (Adjunct to this is a supposition that the fair lady is well worth any unreasonable exposure on his part to fortitude and danger.)

Another allegation, more shadowed and whispered, holds that as rural cowboys witness bovine, canine, porcine, and equine sex, it begins to look like fun. Having ample opportunity to participate, they ultimately do so, acting out their fantasies with passion and glee atop the poor dumb female beasts. Sows and ewes are alleged to be the preferred rapees in this orgy but by no means the only ones.

All the above have been overgeneralized to the point of myth. Not one is true. The rural cowboy is no more and no less tasteless, gross, or reticent in his sexual conduct and no more confident or skillful than is the mean of male juveniles wherever they may live.

One shouldn't read into this, though, that environment fails to strongly affect sexual attitudes and appetites on the range. The Luna Kid and his sexual metamorphosis is a case in point. While certainly not typical, his experience would appear fairly ordinary if it had not been so highly colored by the idiosyncrasies and isolation of the village in which he lived and loved. That, plus the times.

There were no naked centerfolds in those days, no sexy calendars or X-rated movies. (Indeed, movies were not allowed to show male and female on the same bed, whether seated, standing, fully clothed, or otherwise.) Occasionally, the rural cowboys would pass around from *True* magazine a Betty Grable pinup, showing her lovely thighs pressed as tightly together as Eleanor Roosevelt's lips. Or *Look* would include a nighty-clad pose of some breasty, long-legged starlet. It was all slightly provocative but hardly the stuff to arouse active and hardworking rural cowboys. Those juvenile cowboys didn't need much stimulation anyway. They already had, in every home, about all the titillation that could readily be borne by hot, young, testosterone-laden males.

They had mail-order catalogs.

It was Sears, Wards, Penney's, and the like, that first introduced most rural cowboys to the wonders of the flesh, at least flesh in print. With boys in the house, the pages of ladies' underthings were likely the first to be fingerprinted in each new catalog. And when that catalog was typically relegated to the outhouse for toilet paper, the surviving underwear pages would predictably be the last used up. Next in popularity among many rural cowboys were the sheer stockings, then sleepwear, followed by girdles, garter belts, and swimsuits. Those rural cowboys with more kinky sensuality would often be drawn first to the section on bras (especially "full figure" ones). Even foundation garments appealed to some erotic young eyes. Indeed, one of the Hickam boys of Round Valley became known ever after as Pregnant Charlie when somebody caught him ogling a Wards sale catalog on maternity underwear and playing with himself.

The Luna Kid was more oriented toward female legs than to any upper anatomy. Thus, it was the stocking sections, before any others, that drew his prurient attention. He especially enjoyed pictures of legs without heads, because he could always think of a pretty head and torso that perfectly matched each pair of legs. If the pose was especially provocative and an entire model was depicted, he would sometimes just cover the face and let his imagination substitute a familiar one. Thus, many a local girl or young woman, married or not, eventually exposed her legs in a pair of Sears stockings to the hot fantasies of the Luna Kid.

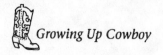

Others of the rural cowboys were wont to fantasize about their usually young, female school teachers. Perhaps relationships between boys and teachers are more elemental in villages than in cities. In a two-room school, a teacher cannot easily withdraw into haughty isolation the way she does in larger schools. Thus, she is more likely to be viewed and treated as one of the boys, or more correctly, by the boys as "one of the girls" who happens to have nice, big, curvy legs (rural cowboys hate skinny, straight legs) and a mature body.

Miss Curry, about age twenty-three, was such a specimen. Even though she dressed severely in an attempt to hide it, she was sleek as a filly, seeming all leg and haunch. And she had big, grey, oh-so-feminine eyes set wide apart in a pristine white face. It was well known at school, and often complained about (by girls), that she liked boys better than girls. She tended to help the boys more and discipline them less, a fateful trend that the rural cowboys eventually took advantage of.

They rather perversely began to tease poor Miss Curry. For example, they delighted in snowballing the girls' outhouse to keep her inside. Once she was in there, ten or twelve of the boys would launch such a barrage against the outhouse door that she couldn't possibly open it to come out without risking a thorough powdering and perhaps some painful bruises, especially if Googy was among the snowballers. Googy may have been held back. He was oversize and overstrong. He dwarfed the other rural cowboys and might have intimidated and bullied them except that he was compulsively cheerful. But you didn't want to get hit by a snowball or anything else thrown by Googy because he was just as powerful as any mature cowboy in town.

At the school picnic that year, Googy, cheered on by the kids, picked up Miss Curry and carried her across Frisco

Creek. He seemed strangely flushed when he put her down, and the Kid thought maybe Googy had discovered with his hands what the other rural cowboys had discerned with their eyes: Beneath all those duds there was a lot of soft, sexy woman.

Soon, as always, wrestling broke out among the macho rural cowboys, who never missed a chance to show off. But it ended quickly when word got around that Googy had decided to wrestle Miss Curry. That was no contest. The entire class gathered, laughing, cheering, and clapping, as Googy simply picked up a blushing, protesting Miss Curry, tripped her gently onto her right side in the grass, laid his bulky body across hers, and refused to get up. One hour, two hours, the entire afternoon passed, and Googy wouldn't get off Miss Curry. His position changed, though, as the afternoon wore on. They wrestled around until finally she was flat on her back and Googy came belly to belly on top of her in perfect missionary position. He seemed to enjoy it without quite knowing why.

At first Miss Curry giggled and laughed in the spirit of the outing. But after ten minutes or so, she was telling Googy: "Okay, that's enough. Help me up." And later: "Now, I'm serious. Get off me at once." She finally got down to her sharpest reprimanding voice. "Young man, this has gone way too far. Get up this instance, or you'll be in a lot of trouble."

The more she protested, the more Googy would wriggle around on top of her. Finally, she began to beg Googy to remove himself. He wouldn't get up. She wept. He wouldn't get up. Toward the middle of the afternoon, some of the girls took pity on Miss Curry and began to berate Googy for his heavy-handed rudeness. Two of them tried, without success, to pull him off, all the while castigating the grinning, standing-around rural cowboys for complicity and cowardice.

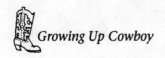

Along late in the afternoon, Miss Curry, who had lain quietly for nearly a half-hour refusing to speak to Googy, raised her head to call Vera over and whispered in her ear. Vera whispered something angrily to Googy. He flushed and lay back flat on Miss Curry for maybe two minutes then suddenly, without a word, propelled himself off her and stalked away into the woods. Vera and Miss Curry went off in a different direction.

The infamous laying-on episode was over.

Later the rural cowboys pumped Googy for his sensations while languishing atop Miss Curry. "Right where her belly ends and her legs begin, I could feel a hollow," he confided. None of the aspiring rural cowboys doubted that an awesome cavity existed in that area. But each added his own interpretive twist to this new, almost frightening information. In fact, Googy's description sorely misled the Kid as to both the location and the shape of the crucial feminine anatomy. From what Googy said, Kid imagined a gaping hole, boring straight back toward the rear.

A couple of years later, in his earliest attempt at sex, the Kid positioned himself accordingly and thus, to his keen disappointment, merely ravished in the darkness the smooth dry crease between a pair of thighs. His confusion was exceeded only by the intense disgust of his partner, who let libelous word get around among the several rural cowboys with whom she promiscuously and regularly carried on that she was through with the Kid because "he don't know how."

She was talked into giving the Kid one more chance. This time, his manhood failed to achieve the necessary extension even to reach her inner thigh. So his friends condescendingly kicked the Kid out of their gang-bang Trudy club.

Resolving that the real thing was no fun anyway, the Kid turned back to the stocking section in the catalog.

Then one day, while burying refuse left behind at the ranch by some hunters from Texas, he came upon a tattered nudist magazine. The photographs not only took his breath away, they taught the Kid a lesson in female anatomy. After an exhilarating then clinical study of the photographs, he figured he finally knew how, so he resolved to go out and get his own sex. He'd show the rural cowboys that there was something better than gang-banging Trudy in the dark. He'd go after the one with the biggest, curviest legs, the one they all wanted to get their hands on.

The Kid would seduce Dia Felt.

* * * * *

At dusk, the Kid shows up along the road in front of Dia's place. He hangs around outside the fence until she comes out.

"Annalee and some others are gonna parch corn on the mesa. Wanta go?"

She smiles at the Kid. It's a sexy smile. "Sure. Just wait 'til I change."

Dia is not as pretty as several of the other girls. But she has some nice features. Her forehead is high and curving. Her eyes are light blue and real bright. Her mouth is small, and it puckers a little when she closes it. That's one reason the rural cowboys think she's sexy. She really doesn't need that extra sexiness, because she gets good grades, and any girl who gets good grades, and has good legs to boot, is just automatically sexy. Kid doesn't know why. Maybe it's because Trudy, who lives in another town, doesn't go to school and she's not too bright. Even though she gives them sex, none of the rural cowboys ever thinks of her as sexy. The Kid figures that any girl who gives just anybody sex is definitely not sexy.

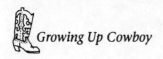

Dia is different. She's as pure as spring water. But she has sex, alright, and the Kid knows from listening to the big boys that any girl will give you sex. All you have to do is approach them right. Make 'em hot. Yes. Luna Kid has a plan to make Dia hot.

Dia comes out in rather loose-fitting slacks and a sleek blouse that buttons down the front. Her hair is drawn back in a ponytail, making her face stand out. Except for a row of freckles down either side of her nose, her face is shiny, almost waxy. She bears a cheery smile, and her eyes are even brighter than usual. The Kid can tell she is glad that he came by for her. He is fairly sure she's never been out with a boy; maybe she is already a little hot from thinking about it, same as the Kid.

They walk down the road to where a lane cuts up toward the mesa by the graveyard. Dia doesn't say much. She's known as a little on the quiet and shy side. But she claps and says, "Hey, good shot," when the Kid throws a rock and knocks a can off a post. They walk on through knee-high weeds, stepping around thistles and trying not to scrape against the milkweed, which causes stains.

The ditch is full of water. Kid jumps across and turns, expecting Dia to do the same. Instead she extends a hand. It is pale and pretty with long drooping fingers. He takes it and feels its softness. She jumps across with a squeal. As she lands, a leg brushes against the Kid. Now he's sure she's getting hot, holding out her hand and rubbing against him that way. The Kid feels choked up. He doesn't let loose the hand, and she doesn't object. Now they're holding hands. That's the first thing to do. His mind goes over the seducer's checklist: Next you put your arm around her. Then you kiss her on the cheek several times. After she gets a little hotter, you kiss her lips, then her open mouth. Then you touch your tongue to hers. That'll really get her going. After a while, you play with her tits from the outside; then you go inside the dress and feel around under her bra and down around her belly button. It's best to play with her legs before you go after her crotch. When she spreads 'em, you go in. Kid has learned, too, that there are lots of little side tricks you can use to advantage on girls. Sometimes tickling is the best way to get 'em passionate and ready. What's more, Red Piersall has got several girls hot enough to "kiss a rattlesnake," just by telling them dirty jokes.

The Kid and Dia come up to Casey's pasture fence. Kid climbs through gingerly and holds the barbed wire strands apart for Dia. She stoops, slips through, legs parted, then stands beside the Kid. "Gee, you're a gentleman," she declares. "But for that, I'd have tore my pants half off."

The Kid savors the innuendo. His manhood is rising. She's practically begging for it. He puts an arm around her shoulders as they walk on. She answers with an arm around his waist. It is coming on dark. An owl is hooting just beyond Trout Creek. They walk along quietly. Bluebirds flutter out of the weeds ahead. Now they see the bonfire just across the wash. Kid's heart is pumping. He can hardly believe his luck. This Dia is hotter than anybody would've believed. It's only a matter of time.

"I betcha you don't know," says the Kid in a little bit of a shaky voice, "what the old hen said when a truck ran over her."

Dia raises her eyes to his in surprise. "Did you say 'hen'?" she asks.

"Yeah. Old hen."

"Silly," her hand tightens at his waist. "Chickens don't talk."

"You think that's what she said?"

"No. That's what I said."

"Well, I was just kiddin'."

"Oh."

They walk on toward the bonfire. Some kids are

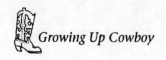

already gathered there. Finally, the Kid asks, "Well, dontcha want to know?"

"Know what?"

"What the old hen said."

"Said when?"

"When the truck run over her."

"Okay. What?"

"She said, 'Boy howdy! That old rooster sure was rough.' Heh, heh." The Kid snickers.

She looks up again, puzzled. "What's funny?"

"Well, ah." The Kid is flustered. "The hen thought it was a rooster. Ain't that funny?"

"Why would a rooster drive a truck over a chicken?"

"He wouldn't. Dontcha see? That's the point."

"What's the point?"

"That the old hen thought a rooster had, ah, taken her. Heh, heh."

"Taken her! Where to?"

"Oh, well, don't worry about it. It's just a story."

Dia giggles then and tugs against his waist. She stops him and they turn toward each other. "Sure it's funny. I'm kinda dumb, you know." She has a hand softly on either side of his waist. "I'm just surprised the truck never killed the old hen."

The moon has come up behind the bonfire. The fire and the moon shine together on Dia, imparting a flicking yellow glow to her forehead and illuminating her puckered lips. For a moment the Kid forgets his mission. Those lips, he's never seen a sight so pretty. Without thinking, he bends his head and kisses her lips. He straightens to find her eyes staring gravely into his. He can tell she is not much affected by the kiss. Maybe even didn't like it. He silently cusses his impatience. You're supposed to work up to kissing on the lips. Now he'd put the cart before the horse, and she hadn't been ready.

Tough field corn is already roasting on the coals as Dia and Kid join the gang at the bonfire. Kid is thinking that he's had a setback. Now he's gotta get down to basics. Just wait 'til the fire dies and they commence roasting marshmallows. He'll go to work on Dia again. He's sure to get it tonight. He'll get her hot enough to pop, and . . . on the way home and right in the weeds!

Dia is sitting on a log back in the shadows. Kid comes up behind her and presses his fingers against her ribs on each side. She gives a ritualistic squeal and giggles, "You never scared me. I heard you comin'." His fingers press against the sides of her chest, then move upward. She doesn't respond or even grow tense. His hands come up under her elbows.

"What you doing?" she asks, nibbling on an ear of corn.

"Uh, well," answers the Kid, "I was just seein' if you're ticklish."

"Not a bit," says Dia, and she raises both elbows, giving the Kid full access to her armpits.

Another setback, but the Kid has gone too far to back off now. He kneels behind her and slides both arms across her chest. It's as flat as his own. He feels a protrusion against the pulse of his right wrist. It must be her left tit. He moves his fingers to fondle there. It is erect, hard. It is a button on her blouse. His groping hand moves on across and finally feels a nipple beyond the fabric. It's like the eraser on a pencil. He has to stroke with some care because he keeps losing it. With his other hand, he finds her right nipple and strokes that too. Now he's really giving her the business.

Dia continues to nibble on her parched corn. She doesn't seem to mind Kid stroking her. But why isn't she heating up? From what he's learned, the nipples are supposed to be stabbing at his palm by now, but they still only feel like erasers. Worn erasers at that.

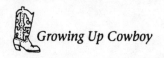

Kid's hands drop to slide across her stomach. She tenses a little for the first time. Then one hand moves to her leg about midway between knee and thigh. Dia seems to shrink away as if the sensation is unpleasant. She abruptly stands and twists, causing the Kid's hand to brush away.

Again the Kid swears at himself for being impatient. Should have worked longer on the tits. He follows her back to the dying fire. She impales a marshmallow on a stick and holds it out to the embers. The night is now quite dark. The rural cowboys are dispersing. Most of them will walk home in a group with the girls. The Kid is the only one who has a girl of his own and a chance to make out.

The Kid and Dia kick dirt over the embers. Dia has had a good time—she's happy and flirting, kicking dirt on the Kid and giggling. Then they sit on the log. The stars are brilliant overhead, but it's getting cold without heat from the fire. Dia is sitting close to the Kid. He has an arm around her. He is busy with her tits. He doesn't dare reach lower because he's afraid she'll stand and twist away again. She's just bound to be hot now. All he needs to do is ask her for it. She'll say, "I guess so," and pull down her pants. They'll do it right here in the sand. But Kid can't decide what to say. He'll wait a while. She'll get hotter.

After a while, Dia stands. "We'd better walk toward home," she says. The Kid's manhood rises. That means she knows a place where she wants to do it, he reasons. On the way, he'll ask her.

Their arms are around each other as they walk down the starlit lane. Dia is happy, even a little giddy as they now and then push against one another with their hips. Again she stiffens as she climbs back through the fence and Kid reaches a hand to her legs. But she doesn't object when she jumps across the ditch into the Kid and he clutches her and kisses her repeatedly on the mouth.

They turn up the dark deserted street at the end of the lane. They still have an arm around each other, and the Kid is brazenly fumbling across the front of her chest with his free hand. Gotta keep her hot. But now they've passed up most of the good places to do it, and the Kid is getting desperate. He's got to put the question. For sure, by now, she's burning to hear it.

In the distance, her house looms against the starry sky. Its windows are dark. Just across the fence is a woodshed. The last place. The Kid's heart is pumping against his eardrums, and there's a lump in his throat. His manhood has been rising as each step brings them closer to the dark, yawning front of the woodshed.

Dia is a warm and sensual presence there beside him. He feels a deep-down choking longing for her. He must possess her. Now is the time.

Ah, but how does one pose this, the question of the ages? To what combination of words and symbols does a virgin unlock her body?

"Change in a trice/The lilies and languors of virtue/For the raptures and roses of vice. . . . " So begged a lover of Swinburne's Delores. And somewhere in literature is this supplication from a shepherd to a maiden: "Come live with me and be my love;/And we will all the pleasures prove . . ."

But the Luna Kid has run out of time. He has no words for romance or thought for whispered innuendo. With his arm around her and hers around him and the woodshed coming close to passing behind them, he must communicate, and the time is now or never.

Through the dryness in his throat, in a voice that seems apart from himself, as though a third party has come to speak to her, he blurts up and out into the cool darkness, "Dia, how about a piece of ass!"

Dia's chin and arm drop as suddenly as though a bullet has struck her temple. In an instant she's only a

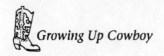

figure ahead of the Kid, walking swiftly through the night toward her house. She doesn't raise her head. At the gate she's nearly running and four or five steps ahead of the Kid.

The Kid stops. He watches her through the gate, up the walk, across the porch. Her head is still hanging. She hasn't said a word or made a sound. He hears the door as it closes quietly but firmly behind her.

It's a cold walk home. The Kid doesn't pay attention to where he's walking and stumbles several times on windrows of gravel at the center of the road. He's hoping he won't see Dia tomorrow, maybe never again. If she tells anybody, he'll just deny it, that's all. But won't that make her a liar? It wouldn't be fair to let a decent, fine sweetheart of a girl like Dia look like a liar, especially now that he knows who the liars really are.

Good to have that knowledge. Gives you a feeling of freedom. He skips along atop the windrow, somehow relieved, nearly happy. Eases your mind. Kind of takes the pressure off.

6

Let a
Dead Horse Rest

Because World War II depleted the countryside of workers, rural cowboys of Luna Kid's generation had to grow up a little quicker than most. Though mere boys, by the time the war was in full swing, their feet were iron soled from barefoot summers of years past. Their legs were already bowed from sitting in the saddle, and they were knobby kneed from crawling along potato fields. Their necks were stiff and freckled from following the walking plow. They'd grown tough as rawhide, figured they were ready for anything, and viewed themselves as men, not boys.

The Luna Kid was a member of this gifted class.

They'd learned to use an axe, a crowbar, and a pitchfork. They could take a rasp and pinchers and shoe a horse, knock over a buck at 200 yards with a .30-30, tend a thresher, and doctor a cow. They could stretch wire with a pinch bar, harness and hitch a team, spin-crank a jitney, and double-clutch a truck. They were so macho they'd test for

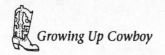

life in a magneto, or kill an engine, just by grabbing the spark plugs. They could handle just about any task, they thought.

That was before they came up against the ultimate challenge, the separator, a tool to sort out the men from the boys.

In the early war years, local folks built a couple of small sawmills. About that time, some gaunt, rawboned "Arkies" moved into town, bringing with them a gadget the rural cowboys had never used. For want of a better term, one might call it the Arkansas crosscut. It looked simple enough—a six-foot steel strip with alternating teeth and depth gauges. Oh, they'd seen little two-man saws before, but this one was different. Like a big fish or fat man, it was deeper in the middle than at either end, heavy as a doubletree, and sharp as bobcat fangs. It was also the most diabolical instrument ever invented with which to torture a body.

The rural cowboys watched those Arkies use that big, strange, shiny crosscut. The saw flowed back and forth, silky smooth, effortlessly, as though mounted on roller bearings. And each stroke vomited forth a stream of sawdust and shavings while sinking the saw another half-inch into that sweet-smelling ponderosa.

Here was a way to make some money. Kind of glamorous, too, bringing down those big trees, hollering "TIMBER" and all. And it got you out in the fresh air, away from the smoky, noisy sawmills. Mere child's play, this. The saw practically ran itself, and they paid you three dollars a thousand just to get those logs ready for skidding. His two older brothers contracted immediately and enlisted the Kid to carry the water bag and wedges and to fill in on the saw in the unlikely event that one or the other should grow weary of the trifling task.

That was the illusion, but the reality was something else again. One doubts whether God or man has ever invented a more difficult way of earning three dollars than cutting down and bucking up a thousand-board-feet equivalent of pine timber with that devilish Arkansas crosscut. . . .

* * * * *

They have barely notched the first tree before Dave, red-faced and panting, thrusts the handle at his end into the Kid's eager hands. He bends to the task. One pull, two pulls, three pulls. His back, twisted forward and corkscrewed to one side, is hurting. Four pulls, five pulls. It is like dragging a roped calf across a muddy corral. More pulls, back hurting more now. Arms aching, chest burning. The saw has penetrated only a couple of inches, and Lamar is growling: "Durn it," his voice winding down into a series of breathless grunts, "yur ridin' the saw. Cut it out."

"Ain't neither." Pant, pant. " 'Taint me, it's you."

They saw on. Sweat drips across the Kid's glasses so he can't see the trunk of the tree. Are they even half through? There's a granny knot in his spine, and his legs are numb. "Maybe the saw's pinchin'," he gasps, hoping Lamar will stop to check.

"Naw, yur just ridin' it," Mar insists.

From the shoulder down, the Kid's arms feel dead when Dave relieves him. He lies on the ground to catch his breath. They stop sawing, and Mar gets attention by delivering a firm kick against the fleshy part of the Kid's thigh. "Git up."

"What's wrong?"

"You're laying where the tree's gonna fall."

He scrambles out, and they hear a rasping, tearing crack, then a louder one. The tree hinges over, and they stand silently watching it. Not one of them has enough breath or energy left to yell "timber."

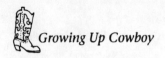

They're just getting started, and they're tired already. They mark the trunk into sixteen-foot segments and attack it again with the crosscut. It goes great, the way the Arkies demonstrated, slicing down five inches, six, but the sawdust is turning from coarse to fine, and Kid's brothers are beginning to grumble at one another for riding the saw. Kid thinks maybe the saw is pinched and pounds in a wedge. It strikes the steel and binds the saw. His brothers cuss him good. He spells Mar. The saw sticks. They jerk it back and forth, Dave and the Kid, accusing one another. Finally, they pull the saw out. Its center section is coated with pine gum. They siphon some gas from the old truck, pour it over the gum, and start sawing again.

The saw pinches. They try to come up from below. The saw handles are too long. They start another parallel cut from the top, and soon that pinches. They reverse the handles on the blade and start from the bottom of the log again. Now they are holding up the weight of the saw, pressing it against the wood, and pulling. It is like carrying one calf across a muddy corral while dragging the other. Finally, the saw cuts through and the log drops free. They measure it, taking their time because they need the breather. Maybe 180 board feet. They look at the sun. It's about eleven. Three rural cowboys have worked four hours and made six bits.

There's no record of how many days or weeks or months they cut timber with the old crosscut. Later the Luna Kid recalled with clarity only the first day and the last. All the time in between could be reckoned mainly in soreness, exhaustion, and tedium.

They got better at it as time went on, but not much better. Their wind and muscles got stronger, but not much stronger. Finally, they made a little more money than on that ill-fated first day, but not much more. They probably would have quit soon anyway, even if they hadn't been put out of business by a calamity that seemed like an act of God at the time and no fault of their own. On the other hand, one of those clever old Arkie lumberjacks wouldn't have gotten into the pickle the rural cowboys did.

* * * * *

They are cutting in big pines out somewhere along the old road that used to go past Yankee Bland's place down toward the Dry Blue. The ranger has marked a towering ponderosa, big at the base and straight as a pole. Looks like a couple of thousand feet in that one tree, and $6 for them. They attack it greedily. Because the behemoth has no lean in any direction, they notch the west side, figuring it will be easier to buck if it falls across a little swell. They've gotten cocky about drawing trees, having learned how from the Arkies.

They begin to saw. Spelling one another, they cut right on through that big fellow to a position above the notch. It doesn't fall. They sledge in two wedges. It doesn't fall. They warily cut both sides on a diagonal above the notch. It doesn't fall. They saw all the way to the top of the notch. It doesn't fall. There isn't a sliver of wood holding that tree, but the cussed thing won't go down. They hammer in two more wedges, and suddenly the tree creaks and settles back on the saw and wedges just the way you'd slip into an easy chair.

The rural cowboys whirl and run in three directions. Finally they gather, panting, outside the lethal perimeter, and look back at the tree. It stands, proud and tall. A little breeze commences. The tree doesn't fall. They wait, staring, for some reason whispering. The tree seems to stare back, angry and ominous. Finally, Kid's brothers elect him to retrieve the axe and the water bag, their only tools not trapped between the ten-ton log and its stump. He creeps

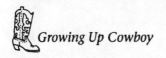

in, and tiptoes out again, as though that big ponderosa is a hibernating grizzly. They wait. It doesn't fall. They yell at the tree. They pelt it with rocks. It doesn't fall.

What can you do? They crank the old truck and head home for dinner.

It's been said a falling tree doesn't make noise when there are no ears to hear it. Nobody knows when that big ponderosa finally lost balance and crashed to the ground: There were ears in the vicinity all right, but they wouldn't have heard a thing.

The rural cowboys retrieve their saw next day. It has a permanent crick along its steely spine, similar to the one the Luna Kid received from the hours and days spent riding (so his brothers insist) on the end of it. Its days are done. This particular Arkansas crosscut will torture no more.

They pack away their wedges and make room for the goosenecked saw. Herbert Bastion can fashion some dandy pocket knives out of it.

Lamar and Kid are cranking the jitney when Dave calls them over to the fallen tree, near the crown. They part the needles and look where he points. There lies the carcass of a horse, sandwiched peacefully between the branches and the stony ground. It is a nice blaze-face bay, a familiar gelding around Luna. A good looker. They stare silently. Kid is thinking, "There, but for the grace of God, lies Daddy's number four son."

Finally somebody says, "I don't know that horse."

"Me neither," the others echo the little white lie.

They stare some more. After a few minutes, Dave speaks up. "I betcha one thing."

"What's that?"

"That there pony sure never knew what hit him."

And neither, to this day, does his owner.

The rural cowboys were still in their teens when they retired permanently from the log woods. Maybe they were born too soon. If somebody had invented the gas chain saw a couple of years earlier, they might still be lumberjacking.

7

Downfall of the Great White Trapper

M other Nature may be a wondrous designer, but she has also brought a few lemons to life's assembly line. Even her crown jewel, the Homo sapiens, seems in some ways to have been "picked a little green," as they say. More time on the test track might have revealed the kinds of flaws, easily corrected in design phases, that are all but impossible to fix at a later date.

In any new model of people, for instance, Nature would almost certainly want to reconsider the matter of outside trim and decoration. Among land mammals, only man has come out hairless and unadorned. This slight has proven both fateful and woeful to the most beautiful birds, beasts, and reptiles of the Earth. Nature's greatest error in design was to let loose, among herds of attractive and colorful animals, just this one that was homely, hairless, unadorned, self-serving, and deadly.

The inevitable trouble began when shivering primitive man swiped skins off other animals to warm his body.

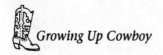

Later on, he noticed that those creatures were prettier than he was, so he decorated himself with feathers and furs to establish equality. So far so good. Nature could live with this. The borrowed coats and dress-up stuff were just by-products of the struggle for existence. It wasn't until man became civilized and vain that the worst-case scenario came to pass. That's when he began killing innocent animals for their skins only, just to show himself off to others of his own kind.

When early man needed a coat from an animal, he usually killed the bearer with projectiles. But the vanity to come would not tolerate bruises and holes in the pelts. Needed was a way to capture the bearer without harming the fur. Thus was born the steel trap, not only sparing the pelt, but mechanizing the operation as well. It greatly leveraged the business of providing fur pelts, for it allowed an animal to be taken at the convenience of the hunter.

Homo sapiens would now collect from the wilds, with little effort or danger, the loveliest bounties of Nature. True, the skinee might have to wait there in the trap for a few days before giving up its pelt, but what is time to an animal?

With the coming of the steel trap, mankind's revenge for the homeliness of his heritage could express itself in the perverse poetry of civilized justice. Merely to humiliate by death those creatures more handsome than he had fallen short of erasing his envy. Now they were to suffer as well. Accordingly, during the war years of the forties, the Luna Kid, too young to fight the gun-toting Japs and Huns, would set out to do his patriotic duty by going after the fur-bearing animals.

But that's a little ahead of where the story starts.

There are additional reasons for trapping animals. Some rodent pests used to be most easily exterminated by trapping. Such animals, as one might imagine, had deeply penetrated the woods, stumps, rocks, and fields of the Upper Ranch. And they had come to view the oats Daddy planted there as if the harvest were their own.

The Kid wasn't even out of bib overalls when he made his first money as a trapper. Daddy would pay a nickel for each tail of a gopher or chipmunk he brought in. All he needed to do was find a fresh gopher mound, dig away the soft dirt to expose the hole, and set the trap. An upright plate held apart two spring-powered levers that would instantly fly up and skewer any gopher who pushed against the plate. Chipmunks were caught in a small trap equipped with conventional jaws. The Kid would set it at a hole in a stump or rock and bait it with grain.

* * * * *

"Where to so early?" Kid's mother knows he hates getting his pants wet with dew. Generally he hangs around the cabin until the sun has dried the weeds and grass.

"Check my traps."

Mother frowns and shivers. She doesn't like the idea of Kid's trapping.

Kid is wet to his knees by the time he comes up to the first gopher trap. He's excited and ready. Lamar's pocketknife presses against his leg. He's borrowed it to cut off tails.

The first setting has been disturbed. There's new dirt above the trap in the hole. Kid tugs at the chain. The trap has been sprung. He pulls it out and thrills to the sight of a dead gopher there. He opens the trap and shakes the gopher off. Kid hears it hit the ground with a cold thud. He opens the knife and kneels there over the gopher. It's a little animal with sleek fine hide, but its tail is coarse like dog hair. For a thing that lives in dirt, the gopher is perfectly clean, as if fresh scrubbed.

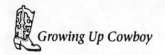

The dirt in the hole, up there in front of the trap. Where'd it come from? Maybe the answer could be seen on the little body. Maybe the springing spears caught back in the belly instead of stabbing quickly through the heart. Kid doesn't want to look anymore.

He has the tail. That'll bring a nickel. Heck of a lot more than any little dirt grubber is worth. That face. It's a picture of peace there. Eyes closed, no sign of pain. But the white underside is bloody. The gopher had fought with its last breath to close off its own grave, Kid's two steel hooks imbedded there in its belly.

Kid enlarges the hole, and drops the gopher back inside. It's the same gopher as before except the tail is gone and it's not breathing. That breath will soon be a nickel in Kid's pocket. Confounded critter. It shouldn't have struggled there. A cussed gopher oughtn't to make a big deal about dying. Its sorry life sure wasn't worth struggling there and pulling those spears even deeper into its belly.

Kid sits with the dead gopher until the sun is well up and the grass is dry. At last a fly buzzes past the Kid and circles to land on the stubby black nose of the gopher. The Kid brushes it off, gently pushes the gopher deeper in the hole, and tramps dirt in above it.

When the Kid finally stands, his pants legs are coated with dirt where they were wet before. He's dirtier than the gopher, which lies clean except for blood on the white of its belly. Kid has put the tail in his pocket. He imagines it is wiggling like the long white snakes that a wet horsehair turns into. He takes out the gopher's tail. It's not moving, and he doesn't want it any more. He returns to the gopher hole and digs until his fingers touch the carcass buried there. He stuffs the tail alongside the gopher and covers it up again. Seems like he's been digging dirt all day. This trapping gophers is a dirty business. Kid doesn't much care for it. He walks on to check the other traps.

Kid is not ready for the chipmunk. It's a big one with huge, bulging black eyes, and it's cringing down into the trap that has sprung up high around one hind leg. Kid walks around the trap, and the chipmunk writhes ever away from him.

Its terror there in front of the Kid is greater than the pain at its leg, for it is twisting against the caught leg, which vibrates above the jaws, but lies still and motionless below. Kid stops circling the chipmunk, hoping it will lie quietly against the trap. But it twitches and pulls away with a squeak, dragging the trap an inch or so. It's curled into a ball now, tail high.

Kid is careful. He reaches down a foot and kicks the trap onto its edge so the caught leg doesn't bend. He stabs the open blade of his knife against the tail. Nothing doing. The tail moves with the knife. He tries again. Still nothing, and the chipmunk is struggling again. Kid rights the trap and presses his heel down onto the spring. He can feel the chipmunk threshing against his shoe. Kid has a good hold with his toe. He presses. The jaws open. Kid is thinking, what if his foot slips and the jaws crash together again against the leg of the little fellow? Then he realizes the chipmunk is gone. He examines the trap. There's a little hair where the leg was but no blood. He resets and baits the trap. Now he knows what to do.

Over where the fence goes across the Turner draw, he's caught another chipmunk. He lays a curved section of pine bark across the head and body. He grabs at the tail. It keeps flopping out of his free hand. He finally has the hold he wants and slashes hard about halfway up. The tip of the tail comes free in his hand, and there's blood on the knife.

He sets the chipmunk free and watches it scurry toward the fence, half-tail pointing straight up. It is dragging a leg. This one's maybe hurt a little, but its sides heave with breath. And the Kid's the same as got a nickel in his pocket.

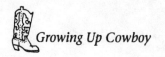

* * * * *

The Luna Kid never set another gopher trap. By July, though, he'd made sixty cents off chipmunks, and there were so many bobtailed ones around that he was beginning to catch them for the second time. Then one day he came up against a far deadlier enemy of the chipmunk than himself. And the experience would forever put the Kid out of the tail-hunting business.

He was setting some traps around a pile of big malpais rocks over near Trout Creek and discovered the half-eaten carcass of one of his bobtailed chipmunks. Kid wondered. A hawk would have carried it off, and a coyote would snap up a chipmunk in a single bite.

Next day, approaching the sets, Kid smells something strange in the air. It is a strong, heavy odor, wild and mysterious, and makes his teeth, as they say, stand on end. If he has ever smelled the stink of danger, this is it.

At the malpais rocks, the trap is gone, and the smell rises even stronger. Then suddenly he forgets the smell, for he hears a dreadful angry hissing and looks directly into two black violent eyes set in a murderous face. He's never seen such a face. The hissing, louder now, is spewing out of a round, red cavern of a mouth, bordered by bright teeth that quiver and slash. Then the red mouth spits fiercely in the direction of the Kid, and the sweet stink comes wafting up again.

It's a dragon there raging at the Kid. The thing is three or four times longer than a chipmunk. Its tail is strangely short, but the neck is half as long as the body. It springs at the Kid, trying to drag the trap. Now it stops hissing and begins snarling.

Kid's first thought is to yell for help. He doesn't know this slashing, snarling, stinking animal. He is breathless. He feels around behind him for a stick, not taking his eyes off the fierce face. In a daze, he holds the stick out toward the face. The dragon attacks the stick viciously with teeth and claw. It lurches again toward the Kid as he swings wildly down across its neck. And though its head lies flattened there on the rocks, it bares the slashing teeth and hisses defiance still, even as the final death blow descends.

The weasel dies quivering.

Kid is as stunned as if someone has laid the stick across his own head. He hadn't told his hands to kill, but there it lies, fur spreading yellow across the back, lightening to the gold of pitch pine along the flank and belly. Kid has never seen an animal so pretty.

Why is he panting? He'd swung the stick only twice, striking back at rage with a rage of his own. But in his heart, the Kid knows why he pants. He is scared, but it wasn't danger that scared him and left him breathless. Call it courage that scared him. For the weasel's snarling spring was the rage of courage, and Kid's answering stick was the outrage of fear.

The weasel lies colorful but lifeless there against the slate-grey malpais. In a way, though, it is not dead to the Kid, for it will come back to haunt his last hour as a trapper. Besides, in years ahead he will ever be watchful of his own kind for the rage of courage. If he sees it or hears it, he will rejoice. And he will remember the yellow dragon.

* * * * *

That fur-bearing animals still get shorn of life and pelt is not exclusively the fault of high fashion. The trapper himself has an interest that is vested not so much in money as in the intoxicating, idyllic quality of his day-to-day life. He tramps with soft hypnotic cadence through a silent wilderness of spicy evergreen. Crossing the ridge and hollow, he reads events of the day in tracks of wild

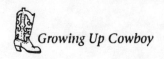

creatures, some of whom are his prey, and judges his luck accordingly. If the sun shines, he glories in it, for the broad leaves are gone. Weeds and grasses do not impede his feet. And there is only himself between the crust of snow and the glorious sky. And if the north wind comes into his face, heavy with the moist foresleet of tonight's storm, he glories in that, too. It somehow makes him feel less of an alien among the animals of this microcosm in which he labors. And it brings his prey to stir out toward the traps, for winter life is most vibrant in the hungry twilight before a storm.

He tramps on, his sets in his mind. They are linked by unblazed pathways known only to himself; they are etched in his mind, for he must know the location of each in relation to the other. Tracks and hovering hawks tell him which sets to approach with most anticipation, but he may not rest his vigil anywhere lest he lose the hidden spot. Clues to each trap are few, only a marker or two in his head—a leaning tree here, a cliff with quartz seams there, a deer trail through the draw yonder. No good trapper could ever describe to another where his traps are set, nor could he make a chart, but his eyes remember when he sees. He tramps on, experiencing and savoring the seeming eternal peace of winter in the wilderness: oak and aspen stripped to trunk and twig, rock and grass mantled in white, the noisy understory of life suspended, asleep in cocoon and egg, even the rot at rest.

And in the early morning of a new snow, new tracks chart another chapter in the course of life around him, for a winter landscape has few secrets. Hesitatingly, as though not wanting to be the first to smear the virgin blanket, the fresh tracks intrude. First, the trapper sees tentative tracings of early risers: a field mouse has struggled out of a tiny, warm cavity and done a diving figure-eight in his own front yard. Why? Who knows. Perhaps the mouse has a secret sauna there under the rocks. A cottontail came up at right angles to the path of the trapper, then hopped off in the direction of two o'clock. A buck crossed the path and walked toward a cluster of junipers to the right. A little beyond, two does and a fawn bisected the trail then preceded the trapper toward the rim of the creek.

By 9:30 the no-longer-virgin snow is everywhere gored by prints of foot and hoof. The trapper has shared space, this day, with two gawky gobblers, for their spiderlike tracks are pressed there in soft snow at his feet. Perhaps to enjoy the sun, a grey squirrel has dashed from a bushy piñon into a barren old oak. Then the first signs of civilization: two unshod horses crossed the ridge toward water at the creek. Jackrabbits and ground squirrels have likewise preceded the trapper, but so far he's seen not a movement of life except the swaying of living twigs when a melting cap of snow has lost adhesiveness and dropped off with a dull plop.

The ridge is crisscrossed with sign now, and the trapper begins seeing some tracks that warm his blood: the raccoon, a pair of ambling shunks, a lone fox (or could it be a small lost dog). Here's a coyote with two pups, and over there a heavy bobcat has pressed his tidy pads deep into the snow. Further on is sign of a smaller bobcat, or maybe it's a ringtail.

The trapper's blood heats, for these are the furbearers. A big coyote, well skinned and cured, will bring thirteen bucks and a bobcat, sixteen. Even a skunk or raccoon will fetch two-fifty, maybe three dollars.

* * * * *

Kid comes up to the creek. The chain of his trap is anchored on the bank, but the trap is set down under water at the muskrat hole. The first two sets are undis-

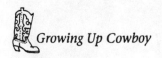

turbed, but Kid excitedly sees a stretched-out chain at the third. Rushing up, he finds a brown muskrat in shallow water near the edge. It's a big one, the biggest yet, and drowned as always. Clean easy way to make a dollar, and now he's caught four of them. Kid isn't sorry for the muskrat, even though it's pretty and has a tail reminding him of that poor little gopher years ago. He's heard that drowning is the easiest way to die.

After checking the muskrat traps, Kid makes his way up a side hollow, where a number-two jump trap is baited with bread. He's yet to catch a raccoon. Maybe today is the day. To his joy, the trap is missing. Kid had tied it to a small branch as any good trapper would do so the coon couldn't jerk loose so easy. He can see where it's been drug away. Figuring the coon is on up the hollow, Kid grabs a stick and runs in that direction. He rounds a bend, jumping gingerly along the rocks, and sees the coon hunched over just ahead. Kid rushes up. The raccoon whirls to face him. It is a little raccoon, not a lot bigger than a house cat.

As Kid approaches, it rises off the trap. One of its hind feet is caught. It spits at the Kid, but there's no fury in its eyes. They are dull with fear, and perhaps pain. Kid can see the white of torn ligaments where the trap clamps.

Executioner and condemned glare at one another in hostile silence. Perhaps it is the Kid's imagination, but the raccoon seems to stretch toward him as though curious or maybe hopeful. Some of the fear is leaving its hooded eyes. There's a sensation in the face like it's about to sniff at him. Kid can wait no longer. With the tentative desperation of one who has come too far, he swings the stick. It strikes a glancing blow at the head. The raccoon cries out. Its handlike paws fly up to cover the hurt. It's over in a searing quarter-second, for Kid's desperation is wild and furious now. He clubs the head repeatedly into the crusty ice and snow at water's edge.

The Kid squats over the snow, his stomach churning. He dreads looking back at the dead coon. But he knows he has to skin it. He owes the raccoon that. Otherwise, all this was for nothing. He takes out his knife, finally, and bends to the coon. He's never skinned one, but he knows how from reading a government pamphlet. He starts a slit at the warm throat. No, he'll wait awhile. He stumbles across the hollow and finds a log in the sun. He sits there for an hour or two before coming back to skin the coon.

Kid is late getting home. Mother is watching for him. "Well, well," she smiles a greeting. "I see you caught a muskrat. And what's the other one?"

"Jist a coon," the Kid spreads out the skin.

"Oh, my," says Mother. "They are littler than I thought." She frowns. "How did you kill it?"

"Whacked it with a stick," says the Kid. "Nothin' to killin' a coon."

Mother's frown deepens, and she opens her mouth to say something. Then she looks sharply at the Kid and closes it again. Finally she says softly, almost sympathetically. "Well, I'm glad you got the skin. Now Daddy'll know you're not just wasting time."

The raccoon is a setback. But the Kid resolves from now on to stand away and use a .22. If he's careful and shoots right through the head it'll die instantly, and a little hole there won't hurt the hide much. Anyway, he'll need the rifle because he has some sets out for skunks. It wouldn't be a good idea to go around clubbing skunks.

* * * * *

Kid has no way of knowing what time of day he caught the skunk. But it's been there for quite a while; that's clear because when he comes up near the trap, two skunks are huddled there together. He's trying to get off a

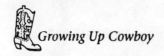

clean shot at a head when suddenly they both run off, leaving the trap behind. He doesn't notice that either one is limping, but when he picks up the trap there's a skunk paw in the jaws and a segment of shin bone. The leg has been severed just as neatly as a beaver chewing down a tree, except the last bit of bone has broken clean. Kid figures both skunks must have been gnawing at the leg all night, maybe taking turns. He shakes the paw out of the trap and buries it. Somehow it seems the right thing to do. Then he makes the rounds and trips all his skunk sets.

On the way home, Kid has a strange thought. He wonders if skunks love one another.

The Kid doesn't tell Mother about the gnawed-off paw, even though he knows she hates skunks. He doesn't tell anybody. That night in a dream he jumps off Dillon Mountain Cliff to get away from a black-and-white-striped kangaroo that is charging him.

Two days later Kid comes up on a whopping raccoon in one of his traps. It seems half as big as a bear, and it is fiercely but painfully alive. It has been attacked by a pack of dogs and has fought back with a great and valiant heart, for dog hair is wildly scattered around the spot. Its fur is the finest that Kid has ever seen, but the hide turns out to be full of jagged holes and is worthless. The skinned carcass is a mess of bloodshot bruises and bites, festered all over. Kid can't imagine anything quite so unfair. He chips a hole out of semifrozen ground to bury the brave old carcass. Wouldn't seem right for it to get bitten anymore. Pity in a way. That big skin would have made an awful nice coat for somebody.

Then Kid makes the rounds and takes up all his raccoon traps. He has had enough of raccoons and skunks along with gophers and chipmunks. From now on he'll only go after calf-killers like wildcats and coyotes. They deserve whatever happens to them. And they're worth more anyhow.

* * * * *

Two carnivores of the Mogollon Breaks are, for all practical purposes, untrappable. One is the mountain lion, which can be baited only with meat of its own killing. Anyway, the mature lion is powerful as a bull. A trap large enough to hold such a beast would be difficult to conceal in the rocky rough-lands where the great cat roams and strikes down its prey.

A second is the bear. Bears can be caught and held, but the huge "bear traps" required can catch and hold a Homo sapiens as well. So obviously, the potential liability in bear trapping today would stagger even Lloyds of London. One legend of the Breaks is of the hunter who stepped into another man's well-hidden bear trap. He became so incensed at the pain and indignity that he unwisely shot and killed the trapper when the latter approached. Thus did two bear predators ironically bite the dust. (The perverse mind may be tempted to envision a circle of bears huddled around the trapped and slowly dying hunter. He yells weakly and swears as the bears howl a dissonant requiem toward the moon and stars.)

For quite different reasons, coyotes are almost as difficult to capture in a trap as lions and bears. "Sly as a fox" is the wrong superlative in the Mogollon Breaks, where foxes are nowhere near as crafty as their swifter and more rangy cousins. Only a few seasoned and likewise crafty trappers can count on a harvest of coveted coyote pelts.

True, the coyote is readily attracted to baits and has an almost suicidal investigative curiosity about each set. But some gifted survivors also seem to possess a mechanical understanding of traps as well as a diabolical insight into the psychology of trappers. Their forte is to provoke anger and frustration by leaving clues that tell the trapper, "I was here, you dummy."

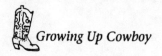

Nummie Brown, an itinerant old trapper, used to claim that some coyotes knew how to spring traps by dropping rocks or twigs on the plate. The Luna Kid wasn't sure he believed Nummie, but from time to time he'd find coyote sets mysteriously sprung, as though a paw had reached around under the jaws to trip the plate. Once a coyote bedded down in snow with his nose only inches away from the Kid's trap. He changed position two or three times during the night, maintaining that distance. Another time, a coyote grabbed the trap by its chain and pulled it right out from under its covering of pine needles. Yet again, with surgical precision a coyote scratched away a layer of pine needles to expose the plate and trigger of a set trap. It was a trick of near demonic defiance, for the slightest pressure on the plate would have sprung the trap. No human would have dared try it, even knowing precisely where the trap was hidden.

By midwinter, the Kid had caught nary a coyote. He decided to borrow some special bait from Nummie. It was the fermented runoff from a tin-floored doghouse, with feces thrown in. Ripened for two weeks in a quart jar under Nummie's wood stove, the goo had taken on, like wine, exotic new aromas each day. A half-gram on a twig could bait a set so potently that, downwind, even a goat would sniff and trot away in disgust.

Still no coyote, only scores of jeering tracks and scratches. Kid took up all his traps, washed them in lye water, then hung them in the smoke of a campfire. Practically guaranteed to kill man-smell. He set them again, and coyotes came, as always. Something scratched up a windrow of frozen dirt to half-cover the trap at one spot. Another coyote, or maybe the same trickster, dropped a fat unfermented turd of its own right on the plate of the next set.

Kid even tried an old trapper's idea of setting an unbaited trap near the first, hoping to trick the sashaying coyote at his own game. This time the coyote sniffed out the bailing wire used to anchor each chain. He uncovered that and a section of chain.

Meanwhile, the Luna Kid caught a bobcat. His trap had been set in rocks on a dry south slope. One day it disappeared without a trace. The kid suspected a big bobcat. He scoured the area but found nothing. Months later while riding horseback on the rim of Trout Creek, he found the bobcat, which had dragged the trap into a grove of scrub juniper and gotten snagged. It died there in the trap. The Kid surely passed within a few feet of him several times during the search. The wildcat skin had shrunk and cracked, exposing a partially bleached skull. Great white teeth seemed bared as if in anger. The once-lovely pelt that might have wrapped a pretty lady was brittle as old paper, its fur crawling with ants.

Beyond shame, Kid didn't even get off Bludog to reclaim the trap. He didn't need it anymore, anyway, for he'd given up trapping one day four months before. A day remembered like yesterday.

* * * * *

He is riding Roanie on a circuit to check the trapline. Spring has brought a warm day. The snow is gone. It's come down to his last chance this year for a coyote. Roanie seems more hesitant than usual. Kid has to keep kicking to coax him up the ridge. There's a trap right on top where two game trails cross at the base of a big alligator juniper. A perfect place to catch a coyote. Roanie seems to hate climbing the ridge today. He seems spooked, too, rearing his head high to stare at the least sign of movement. Strange. Roanie is usually too lazy to give a damn.

They top out finally. The set is just ahead. Abruptly, Roanie stops and flings his head high to stare at the

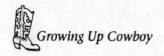

juniper. Kid has a good view ahead and can't see that there's anything in the trap. He swears at Roanie and quirts him on the rump. Roanie at last moves reluctantly ahead. Up closer to the set, Kid realizes it has been disturbed. But the branch he tied it to is about where he left it. He remembers putting extra chain on this trap to get the tie-wire as far away from the trap as possible. Then he sees the chain. It's stretched out toward the trunk of the tree. Something's in that trap.

Suddenly Kid hears a piercing, high-pitched scream. Roanie comes rising off the ground as something brown and wide as a cow shoots from behind the tree and hurls itself directly at them. It screams again right in their faces, but there's a harsh snap of metal. The thing falls to the ground not far from Roanie's front hooves, which are airborne now. Kid can't see what's going on because Roanie's rearing has blocked his view.

It all happens in an instant. Roanie is whirling as he rears. Kid doesn't know if the front hooves have even hit the ground. All he can think of is grabbing the saddle horn to stay on, for Roanie has wheeled around and bolted back down the ridge the way they came. Ducking under branches, the Kid can't straighten enough to bring Roanie under control. The horse charges off the ridge. Kid is struggling to stay in the saddle. Finally off the ridge, he pulls Roanie to a stop.

Kid is scared. He doesn't know what came out from behind that tree. He's not eager to find out either, but he knows he has to. He gets off and ties Roanie, trembling, to a jack pine. You'd never in hell get Roanie back up that hill now. He takes out the .22. Hard enough to get himself to go. Something is caught up there. He took after him and Roanie and would have been all over them except for hitting the end of the chain.

Whatever it is, it shouldn't suffer. The missing bobcat is on the Kid's mind. Even Daddy and the old cow with an ingrown horn. Whatever is in the trap, he doesn't want it. He'll likely have to kill it, and he doesn't even want the thing. That weasel, so many years ago, was easy to kill because he never had to think about it. He just swung the stick when it tried to get at him.

On top of the ridge, Kid is panting. But it wasn't that hard a climb. Up ahead, he hears a rattling. Something is pulling the chain of the trap. He comes slowly up to the juniper. There's movement. His prey has gone back behind the trunk of the tree.

Kid judges the arc of the chain. The thing can charge about twenty feet toward him before the chain stops it. Kid wishes now he'd put on a shorter chain. He's angling around for a look behind the trunk, when it screams again and charges him, dragging the trap. It hits the end of the chain, still raging toward the Kid. The heart of the Kid seems to sink to his knees. It's beating there. And he raises the .22, panting harder.

God almighty. Shades of the weasel. The Kid has caught another golden creature, a huge one, seeming for a fleeting instant bigger than the ridge. It settles back on the chain then and stares furiously at the Kid through witchy black eyes planted at the base of a huge clawlike beak. Kid fingers the safety of the .22. He's never in his life wondered how an eagle might look on the ground. He sure never imagined one would loom so big.

He steps around in a circle. The eagle follows him, dragging the tight chain along. Kid wants to end this. He raises the .22. The head of the eagle comes into the open sights. It is staring at him as though judging a piece of meat, or accusing one, but the look is harshly violent and fearless. Kid isn't panting so now. He's steadier. But he's waited too long.

A powerful coyote trap holds the eagle. If it were a jump trap with only one spring, Kid might have a chance.

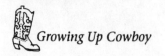

But this has two springs. He'd have to hold both down at once. If he tries to do that, he'll be cut to hell by the beak and free claw of the eagle.

Kid puts down the .22 and brings up two poles. It's hard, sweaty work, causing him to pant again. He snakes each pole out and maneuvers it over a spring of the trap. Then he walks out on the poles toward the eagle, hoping his weight will open the jaws. The jaws slacken a little, but not nearly enough for the big claw to escape. The eagle rages at him. Kid can get no closer.

Kid rolls back the poles and squats beyond reach of the chain. The eagle has stopped surging toward him but continues to stretch against the chain as though determined to protect the piteous little territory allotted to it. One of God's greatest creatures, it is born to a universe of miles endlessly squared. Now it stands fearless like a maddened king in front of the Kid, an alien creature. The king and the alien, they are both trapped and helpless.

The Kid squats beyond the circle of the great bird, his heart shrunken to a hard pounding ball inside. The eagle has to die, he knows, but why? What is the message in this death?

Kid doesn't have to hurry. The eagle appears to feel no pain or fear. Minutes more of its fierce life cannot hurt. So long as blood moves inside the bird and a cold savage reflection shines there in the black eyes, it is the Kid who suffers.

The meaning of this death comes slowly into the mind of the Kid as he squats there under the scathing eyes of the eagle. For too long he has listened outside of himself and tuned out his own soul. It's the same as walking Dia Felt through the weeds of someone else's seduction. The eagle there is like the skunk's chewed-off paw, the raccoon shredded alive, the rotted wildcat tortured and starved to death by the Kid's own hand. They are someone else's phantom catch and yet another's phantom coat. They are not his own.

Now the greatest joke of the young trapper's life stands before him there, waiting for the final futile killing. That is the message of the eagle.

The Kid doesn't dare wait any longer lest he run away from this. The eagle must die, for the time to pay is now. Kid's ball-tight heart seems to knock around loose inside him as he raises the .22. The sooner he can pull the trigger, the sooner he'll be done as a trapper.

The eagle quivers at the end. Just as the weasel did. Kid wonders. These creatures have never known fear. Maybe that quiver is the ebb of rage from deep inside.

He carries the eagle along the ridge looking for rimrock. The great bird is strangely light in weight. Finally he finds a crack in the rocks and drops the body down inside. A hungry bobcat can get in there and have himself a good meal.

As he trots out of Bishop Canyon, Roanie stops and lifts his head high again. Kid is surprised to see a coyote running across the trail about a hundred yards ahead. He pats Roanie on the neck. Kind of heals the heart to see a critter, even a cussed coyote, take off and run like that.

8

Day of the Cougar

R ed Mountain has doubtless been climbed fewer times than Annapurna, Everest, the Matterhorn, or what have you. In fact, there's no record of man ever having scaled it. A possible reason is that Red Mountain does not deserve to be climbed. On the other hand, one could make a logical case that this mountain has not been climbed simply because nobody knows the mountain is there.

The 9,000-foot crest of Red Mountain lies camouflaged. It is not a mountain so much as merely the highest part of Hell Roaring Mesa. To the east it also forms the rim of Bishop Canyon. The floor of the latter lies some 2,000 feet directly below the pinnacle of Red Mountain. Because of its steepness here, the face of the mountain has slid away, exposing naked layers of soft, pink, volcanic ash. Mixed in with this are disjointed and rounded granite stones about the size and color of oranges. These apparently fell from a volcano-blackened sky some millions of years ago. Almost every week, a few of the smooth stony

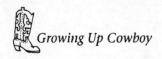

bombs break loose and bounce down toward the bottom of Bishop Canyon, making a noise like wildly running deer. The sound may go on for a couple of minutes as it echoes across the canyon between Red Mountain and Bishop Peak to the east. Higher up, there's a layer of lava much younger than the granite stones. Now and then a chunk of this andesite breaks off to form a huge angular boulder which ponderously begins an eventful descent into the canyon. It takes along rocks or pines or oaks or anything else encountered, and whenever it strikes the ground, it gouges a trench deep enough to bury a sewer.

The east face of Red Mountain, then, is no place for loitering, whether you're human or animal. Even deer trails are scarce. Wild turkeys stroll in and out, but there are few lion or bear signs under the dripping rim. Wary of falling rocks, these powerful, cagey creatures build dens higher up, closer to the andesite cracks and caves.

But there's another face to Red Mountain, and herein lies a story. A minor fork of Bishop Canyon cuts right through the rim of Hell Roaring Mesa, along the south face of Red Mountain. Here the slope is gently terraced by layers of ancient lava and well protected against seasonally frigid southwest gales that blow in from the White Mountains of Arizona. Here, too, the winter sun splashes down, melting ice and snow and warming the rocks across fully a square mile of grassy slope. This is perfect habitat for wintering cattle because there are also springs in the west fork of Bishop Canyon that supply plenty of water after winter snows begin.

You may think that to take advantage of this cow paradise, one merely needs to deploy the cattle. But there's a catch. Cattle cannot be brought in *before* it snows because there's no drinking water then. Cattle can't be driven in *after* it snows because deep drifts block trails across the heights of Hell Roaring Mesa.

Riddle: If Red Mountain can't accommodate cattle before the snow falls, and cattle can't be driven in after the snow falls, how do you ever have cattle there at all?

If you are the father of rural cowboys, and hence their dictator, the answer is superficially easy. You merely decree that, each year, cattle shall be driven across Hell Roaring Mesa and onto Red Mountain in perfect coordination with the first big, howling blizzard of the season. . . .

The Luna Kid wakes slowly to the sound of the radio. It's always dark in the windowless and unheated room where he sleeps. He has to listen for a minute to judge the time. Daddy gets up and turns on the radio at 5:00 every morning; so it's somewhere between then and 7:00 when he generally tromps in and commands the rural cowboys to get up. Then Kid hears the 6:30 news announced from KOB, Albuquerque. That's the only station they can pull despite the fifty feet of outdoor aerial Daddy has strung.

The Kid snuggles back into the warm flannel blankets with relief. He's about to doze off again when he hears the wind outside creaking against the west wall, then whistling around it. Ordinarily the Kid loves to snuggle under the four quilts and listen to the wind, but there's something unpleasant in the sound this time. It's like a bad memory. He dozes, then hears Daddy's boot heels coming across the wood floor. The door opens, and yellow coal oil light shines weakly into the Kid's half-closed eyes. It's too early for that.

"Better git up, son." The Kid winces. When Daddy commands kindly that way, he's about to say something he knows the Kid won't want to hear. "It's fixin' to snow. We'll hafta go to the ranch and drive out the yearlin's."

The Kid doesn't move. It's like if he plays dead, Daddy will go away. He'll miss school, but that's not all bad. A theme is due, and he's not gotten anybody to write it for

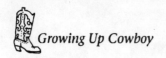

him yet. Ah, the nice warm bus. That's what's bad. It ain't right. He shouldn't hafta be drug out of school for a bunch of durn yearlin's.

"Son," says Daddy in a louder voice. "You hear?"

The Kid makes a demonstration by throwing back the quilts. "Okay, okay," he repeats to himself crossly. It ain't right. Other kids don't hafta do any such thing. Anyhow, he sure doesn't want Daddy thinking he will enjoy gittin' froze feet and pneumonia up on that stupid Hell Roaring Mesa or smashed to smithereens comin' off the side of it in the snow.

"Eat yur breakfast, then chop enough wood fur tonight. We'll be late gittin' in."

The Kid pulls on stiff cold levis. It's like wading out to his waist in ice water. He dresses with three pairs of socks and two shirts. He can barely get his brogans over the socks. He's mumbling darkly and saying "shit" as often and loudly as he dares, hoping Daddy won't be listening but that Mother will hear and sympathize.

At breakfast, Mother is sorry for the Kid. She tries to cheer him up, but he's still cranky. "I'll probably git killed or froze to death out there today," he tells her darkly. As he leaves the table, he adds that he's not about to do any make-up homework either. "Beth's gonna do it. I'll tell you that for sure."

Mother is truly sorry he has to go drive cattle today. She is worried, too. The Kid can see that in her frown. He decides not to say any more. After chopping wood, he comes in out of the raw wind and hears Mother jumping on Daddy for taking him out of school and making a boy do men's work on such a day. Kid sure knows how to get to Mother. But now he's gone too far and caused a fight. Daddy is angrily on the defensive: "Yeah. Well, we'll jist leave them calves up there, and next fall there won't be no steers to sell."

Mother notices the Kid's red nose. "Oh dear, your ears will freeze," she says. On the way out, she slips the sheer top of a cut-off stocking into his jacket pocket. She knows he despises the ugly thing. "Be careful," she says to Luna Kid.

It's starting to snow as they load up and head for the Burke Place at the mouth of Bishop Canyon. The horses are there. They'll have to ride across Hell Roaring Mesa twice today because the yearlings are waiting on the other side and their winter paradise lies on the same side as the Burke Place.

By the time Kid and Daddy are riding up Bishop Canyon, it's nearly 9:00. It's not snowing down here, but clouds hang low over Hell Roaring Mesa, and wind blows down the canyon, feeling damp. Kid hopes the storm hasn't broke on top yet, but it's only a matter of time. From the looks of the sky and feel of the air, the principal may even have to close school early today so buses can get back over the passes to Luna and Glenwood. Most likely Kid would have had a whole afternooon to lie around and read. That's worse luck, especially now with his brothers gone.

Daddy trots ahead about five lengths. Kid has to keep kicking Bludog hard to keep up. Daddy always has a way of making a horse go faster. Bludog is no more eager to climb that mesa than the Kid. They head up the old trail in a steady incline through dull red pines and clusters of fat juniper and piñon. The last half-mile is laced with interlocking switchbacks and brushy with fir and oak and stiff, springy mahogany. The Kid has to stay closer behind Daddy here or rocks might roll down on him and Bludog from the switchback above.

Finally, Daddy stops so Roanie can blow. Kid pulls up behind him. The air is still and heavy. Bludog and Roanie are both winded. Roanie is bigger and slower than Bludog. Generally, the Kid would have to ride the slow horse, but

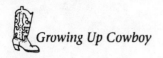

today, for some reason, Daddy has put his own saddle on Roanie.

A light snow begins dusting down. They hear a far-off whistle of wind through the pines beyond the edge of Hell Roaring Mesa. The Kid shudders. He feels lonesome. He only wishes they were headed toward the Burke Place instead of away from it. He's already getting stiff. The brogans don't leave enough room in the stirrup to move his feet around, and the leather leggings are weighting down his legs. On top, he'll be glad to have them turning the wind, though; he knows that. They stop again a hundred yards or so from the top. They can feel the wind now, and it's blowing dry snow under their hats. Kid takes out the cut-off stocking, stretching it over his ears and down as far as he can onto his neck. It looks awful but it's warm. He pulls his hat down until it presses against his ears so it won't blow off the slippery fabric. That's another reason the Kid hates wearing the cussed stocking. He's afraid his ears will get floppy like Hern Slade's because of that pushing down and out against them.

On top, the wind hits hard against the left cheek of the Kid. Daddy stops to put on his own stocking cap. Both horses turn their rumps into the wind while they wait.

They head across the mesa and go on and on. One reason the Kid hates crossing Hell Roaring Mesa is because of its flatness and sameness. You never know where you are. It's somehow like a watch with a dial but no hands. Even the clonelike ponderosas cannot help and only add to the monotony. Kid's feet are tingling, and he dreads the feeling. Soon they'll be burning, almost numb with cold. Maybe Daddy will stop and build a little fire to get warm by. But Daddy doesn't stop. He keeps looking at the sky, and Kid can see he's in a hurry. Snow starts blowing with authority. They ride on, hats and heads tilted sharply to the west and south. Kid's feet are beyond the tingling stage when he senses a break in the trees ahead. He sees the sides of Turner Peak through a white veil. His feet feel leaden, but the west rim is just ahead and beneath that the sheltered little half-valley/half-canyon of the upper ranch.

Wind and snow beat against the high cliffs at the rim as they head down the switchbacks. Kid's cheeks are stinging now, and his nose drips wet spots onto the canvas of his gloves. He hates the swaying as Bludog picks his way down the steep trail. Kid has to keep adjusting, and the cold wind blasts under his chaps and legs. Now even his crotch is cold.

Kid is happy and grateful when Daddy sends him to the cabin to start a fire. It even smells cold and dark in the cabin as he enters, and wind whistles through the chinking next to the rough stone fireplace. But Kid knows he'll soon be warm.

The pine roots take off like a powder fuse with the first match. After a while, when Daddy comes in, he has to warm himself from some distance because the fire is already big and hot. Daddy and the Kid stand there in leggings, quietly warming their haunches as light from the flames throws two fat-legged shadows against the south wall. They nibble at cold dried biscuits from the Dutch oven. Kid can hear calves bawling outside. Daddy has them bunched up, ready for the drive. Daddy tells him that two are missing. Kid's heart sinks.

"They got through the pasture fence," Daddy says. "You'll hafta go find 'em and drive 'em out where that rock gully comes off Hell Roarin' above the allotment fence. There's a gate on top. Once you git through that gate, come on across to Mel's salt trough. From there, follow the draw where we seen that bull elk the lion killed. Keep comin' till you git to the burned-out double snag where Nummie used to set his coyote traps. The old trail crosses right there. Follow that over to Grey Owl Spring, and I'll meet you there with the main bunch."

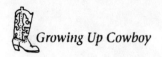

Dread tightens the mouth of the Kid and spreads to make a lump in his throat as Daddy instructs. Daddy always forgets which of his boys knows about these places. But the Kid doesn't have an excuse. He ought to know. He's been there with Daddy. He should have paid better attention. If he asks any questions now, Daddy will point that out. Shit. There's a thousand burned-out snags on Hell Roaring Mesa and all kinds of rock gullies out of Trout Creek. How could Daddy even be sure Kid would be able to find the yearlings?

Maybe Daddy can sense the Kid's frame of mind. "This is a bad-lookin' storm," he says. "We're up against it."

Kid helps drive the main bunch out of the south gate. The grey sky is dropping big lazy flakes. Up to now, they'd melted or blown off, but the ground is turning white in a hurry. Bludog doesn't want to leave Roanie and head up Trout Creek. The Kid is in no mood to humor him. He kicks hard with his brogan heels and cusses. Bludog goes forward through the snow, and he's stepping sideways, his stubby body bent into a crescent to demonstrate his objections.

After maybe twenty minutes of trotting up the creek, the Kid sees the two yearlings eyeing him warily from an aspen thicket. They whirl and run as he rides up. Their backs are damp and wavy. They seem spooked by the storm. Kid follows at a slow trot to save Bludog. They've got a long way to go.

Kid drives them ahead. It's some trouble to turn them up the first rocky gully that appears to climb Hell Roaring Mesa. Their hesitation worries the Kid. The gulch narrows, and its bottom gets rougher. Finally, it boxes in, and the Kid has to drive the yearlings back out again. The snow is coming down faster, and the lump is back in his throat. The yearlings are less frisky now and driving better. They turn themselves up the next gulch. Kid figures that's a good sign because they must know it's a way to the top. They climb a hundred yards and again box out. Kid swears and drives them back out at a high trot. The next gulley is twice as wide. Kid recognizes it with relief. They climb out slowly. The ground and rocks are covered with snow now.

The gate is just where Daddy said. They pass through the fence, and Kid is glad. There's nothing but Hell Roaring Mesa between him and Bishop Canyon now. But the snow is pouring down, and the wind is driving it against his back. At least he's not cold yet. They move across the trailless eternity of Hell Roaring Mesa. The snow is about two inches deep here. Everything but the trunks of the trees is white. Even the air. If there's a trail leading to the salt trough, the Kid can't find it. He's sure they're headed in the right direction because of the slant of the falling snow, but the lump is back in his throat.

He's lost time, and it's running late. They move on a half-hour. Kid is afraid he's already passed the salt lick. The lump grows bigger. Something spooks the yearlings. They veer off to the left, running at first then slowing to a trot. The Kid sees a porcupine angrily slashing the snow-filled air with his mean grey tail. Kid chases the yearlings into a thicket of pines and turns them back. But now they've gone too far the other way. He drives them around a long log then skirts a thicket and then another thicket and another log and heads straight out again. Kid sees some tracks ahead and eagerly overtakes them. There's one horse track and two yearlings. He's gone around in a circle. Kid and Bludog and two yearlings are lost in a dull blanket of snow somewhere on Hell Roaring Mesa.

The Kid is sweating and begins to swear. He swears as loud as he can and pretty soon he's screaming every swear word he knows into the falling snow. Finally, he strains his eyes to see through the thickets and snow. It is useless. Every direction he looks seems like the best way to go. He

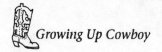

feels smothered by the snow. He pants and gasps. He knows he's close to panic. He begins to curse Daddy in a loud voice. It's sure Daddy's fault if the yearlings freeze to death up here on the mesa. He'd no right to expect the Kid to know his way around in a mess like this. Well, the Kid won't drive these cussed calves another step. He'll just let Bludog have his head and Bludog will go straight to the Bishop Canyon trail they'd come up this morning.

He kicks Bludog wildly and lets the reins go slack. Bludog takes off eagerly in a direction more to the right than the Kid expected. The Kid feels like crying. Daddy's gonna get awful worried. But that serves him right. The Kid is sure going to save his own skin and to hell with the goddam yearlings and to hell with Daddy. Finally, he groans out loud and pulls Bludog to a stop. Bludog wants to go on. The Kid holds him still. There's not a sound except Bludog's breathing and his own gasping and the wind.

The Kid has never felt so lonesome. His mouth and throat pull tighter and suddenly, without expecting to, he begins to cry. He gets down off Bludog, feeling his face contorted. He leans against a ponderosa and presses a thumb over one eye and a forefinger against the other and cries. Finally, in a hoarse voice he says something through his hand into the snow and silence. "Lord, please help me find Daddy. If you will, I won't say no more swear words for at least a year."

After a while the Kid feels better. He gets back on Bludog and kicks the reluctant horse into a trot back toward the yearlings. He is getting an idea. Bludog sure wants to go back to the Bishop Canyon trail. So the thing to do is just give him his head to test the direction. Then Kid will drive the yearlings at about a full square angle off to the left and that oughta be smack dab toward Red Mountain.

The two yearlings have lain down by the time Kid gets back to them. They look at him stupidly through the falling snow. "Git up," says the Kid in a loud voice. It's all their fault. These goddam calves are gonna find out who's boss. The thought only flits through his mind. He doesn't dare say it out loud.

The falling snow is almost blinding when Kid reins sharply from the way Bludog wants to go. They drive the yearlings along in single file. After about a half-hour they come up on the burned double snag. There is no seeing the cow path leading toward Red Mountain, but the Kid knows it is there because of an occasional yellow blaze axed into a pine trunk.

It is along about midafternoon and still snowing when the Kid hears bawling ahead and knows Daddy has beaten him to Grey Owl Spring. His yearlings answer the bawling, and Bludog lets loose a long nicker. The Kid wonders if Daddy is all set to jaw him about being slow. An answering nicker comes back from Roanie, and the Kid hears Daddy yelling at the yearlings to get them on their feet and bunched up again. Kid smells smoke and rides over to where Daddy has built a small fire. He dismounts and holds two gloved hands out to the fire. The gloves are starting to steam when Daddy rides up.

"Ain't this a fright," he says.

The Luna Kid doesn't look up but gazes calmly into the fire. "Shore is, and gittin' worse," he answers.

"Found 'em okay, didja?" asks Daddy.

The Kid looks around. On Daddy's face is the same expression as when he bites into a batch of beans that turned out just right. "Oh shore," answers the Kid nonchalantly. "No trouble at all."

Daddy has the bunch moving right away. He tells the Kid to go ahead and get warm, then catch up, because they've gotta hurry. Daddy's words, yelled through the

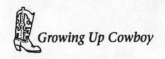

falling snow and over the bawling of the yearlings, break into the peaceful lethargy of the Kid. Daddy is usually more patient when driving cattle. Kid thinks this snow is a little more than even Daddy has bargained for.

The fire is pretty well burned down when the Kid mounts and kicks Bludog into a high trot. The yearling tracks are filling with snow. They drive on.

It is late afternoon when the trees clear away fifty yards ahead. Kid knows they are at the rim. The drive is nearly done. They drop off along the west face of Red Mountain. The storm seems to abate almost instantly, but Kid knows that's an illusion. There's still snow and wind across the mesa. He hates the thought of topping out again to follow the rim back to the old trail they came up that morning.

The yearlings eagerly plunge their way off the mountainside, finding gaps in the rocks to lead them downhill. There's not much snow accumulation here. It's been melting all day. The yearlings are frisky again and happy as hogs.

Daddy tells the Kid that there's too much snow on top to go back along the rim. "We'll hafta go down Bishop Canyon," he says. This news startles the Kid. Nobody uses the Bishop Canyon trail in winter because of ice that stretches across the narrows of the canyon bottom. Maybe that's why Daddy has seemed in such a hurry the whole day. Kid's never been off the canyon in winter, but he knows that ice is nothing to fool with on a horse.

They find the first patch right at the bottom of the switchbacks. Daddy rides ahead. Roanie slips and even before he begins to right himself Daddy has swung smoothly out of the saddle, quick as a sneeze. Roanie stands there gingerly and Daddy tries to calm him. Now the Kid knows why Daddy rode Roanie today. Kid wouldn't have been ready for that slip. If Roanie had gone down with Kid in the saddle, chalk up a broken leg.

"Better git off and lead," says Daddy.

Kid is glad. When you're on horseback, there's a dangerous long way between you and that ice. Anyway, Kid's legs are stiff, and his feet are cold. He needs the stretch.

It's a problem to keep the horses moving across the ice. Bludog handles it more confidently than Roanie. The Kid leads Bludog gingerly on ahead as an example. Roanie keeps slipping. After each slip, he slows down some more. Daddy practically has to drag him along, swearing and jerking. They come to a patch about five feet wide. Rather than step his way, Roanie decides to jump across and nearly jumps over the top of Daddy. Instead he hits him squarely in the back. Daddy goes down cussing and gets up cussing. Kid figures Roanie is in for it now, but Daddy only whacks him with the reins a couple of times and ties them together across the saddle horn. Then he begins driving Roanie down the ice, smacking him on the rump with his hand.

They go a ways, and Roanie abruptly slips, rears, and falls with a grunt, then a pitiful-sounding nicker. At first he just sits there in a kind of shock with his legs under him. Then he slowly rolls onto his left side, stretches out his legs and neck, and flattens himself comfortably against the ice. As Daddy feels his legs, checking for breaks, he raises his head to look. Having ascertained that Roanie's brawny legs are sound as ever, Daddy looks into his face and cuts loose a stream of cuss words. Roanie stares at Daddy with wide, scared eyes for a moment, then blinks and slowly lays his head back on the ice as if to say, "I'm wore out. Call me again when the ice melts."

Daddy yells at Roanie and hits him smartly across the right quarter with a stick. Roanie lies unmoving. Daddy twists his tail. Nothing doing. Roanie lies as if dead. His eyes are open but staring stupidly at the hillside to the west.

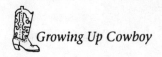

It's snowing harder in the canyon bottom now. Kid knows they have to get moving. There's only an hour or less to dusk.

"Alright, stay here for the winter, you son of a bitch," Daddy rages at Roanie. He jerks off the bridle and unbuckles the cinches. They try to drag the stirrup out from under Roanie, but it won't come. Daddy uncoils his rope and double-hitches it around the horn of Kid's saddle. Then he mounts Bludog and tries to drag the stirrup from beneath Roanie. It's like dancing with a piano on wheels. Roanie slides ponderously this way and that across the ice as Daddy changes the angle of pull. Kid kneels to look pityingly into Roanie's eyes. He expects an expression of terror or maybe humiliation there. Instead, Roanie's eyes are blank and bland as coal. Kid guesses with disgust that Roanie is perfectly content to be lying out on the ice rather than standing over it. If the rural cowboys want to skate him about, that's their problem, not his.

Kid feels sorry for Roanie, but there's something about the scene, if only it weren't so desperate, that makes him wish his brothers were here to see it. They'd be glancing covertly at one another and snickering at poor, clumsy, oversized Roanie stretched out there on the ice and Daddy skidding him about in the white-streaked fading daylight.

Finally, Roanie's broad back stops against a low bank. Bludog strains against the rope. Something gives, then suddenly the stirrup pops free, sending Bludog reeling forward. He rears to stop just short of a leaning tree. Daddy gets off him and strides back toward Roanie. He picks up the saddle. Kid can see red hair and a little blood on the bolt that holds the stirrup to the leather. It scratched old Roanie good coming out. Daddy is looking down at Roanie. Suddenly he yells a piercing "HEEE-YAAW-AAAA" and kicks Roanie hard on the rump. Roanie doesn't even raise his head this time. Kid isn't sure if Daddy is trying once more to get Roanie up or just demonstrating his contempt and disgust. Roanie doesn't move except for his neck, which stretches out a little further. He looks for all the world like a dead horse as they turn away.

Daddy throws his saddle over the Kid's and loops the extra bridle over the saddle horn. They start on down the trail, Daddy walking ahead to find the best crossing over the ice. Kid is leading the horse. It's slow going. At times, the Kid has to pull a stumbling Bludog up the canyon walls to get around downed trees. Once Bludog slides a hoof across his cold toes, and Kid comes close to swearing out loud before catching himself. There's about three inches of snow along here. It's getting colder. The canyon is bleak and spooky in the storm. Kid wishes Daddy would offer to lead Bludog. It's a lot harder work than just walking.

Suddenly, Daddy stops. He is looking down at the snow, then up the canyonside to the right and back in the direction they've come, but high, toward the rim. The Kid joins him and sees cat tracks compressed deeply into the snow. They're nearly as round and as big as Bludog's hoof prints and not a minute old.

Daddy shakes his head. "That's shore a big devil," he says. Kid shudders. They go on, but now Kid is glad to lead Bludog. It's getting along toward dusk, and he's just plenty happy to have some horseflesh bringing up the rear. It's not until they round the bend where the west fork of the canyon begins to open a little, that Kid remembers Roanie with his neck stretched out and catches his breath. A kind of dread comes up out of the pit of his stomach and into his throat. He opens his mouth to warn Daddy, but then he realizes Daddy has thought of it already. That's why he's been peering up to the rim.

It isn't more than five minutes later when the plodding, morose Kid hears a faint, almost musical sound from

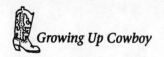

far behind them. Or maybe it's an echo from the bluffs above that he hears because Bludog has already stopped and flung his head around and let loose a long, wild-sounding nicker back up canyon. It echoes twice above them. Daddy stops. He walks back to take Bludog's reins. Bludog is trembling. "We'd better hold him good," says Daddy. "That big lion smells a down horse."

Then they hear again the cry, half-nicker and half-scream, from far up canyon. It is a little louder this time. Bludog bleats a loud but tremulous, almost hysterical, answer. They start out again in eerie silence, Daddy leading Bludog. The Kid brings up the rear feeling heavy of heart and close to crying again. A fleeting thought of saying a little prayer for Roanie crosses his mind, but it's probably too late, and he feels prayed out as well as tired out. Anyway, there's nothing much more to promise the Lord.

At least the damnable drive and the murder of Roanie is over with. Another two or three miles of walking will put them at the Burke Place just before dark.

It's snowing harder when they drop down into the main canyon and find the well-used fire trail. The going is easier here and more familiar to the Kid. He's been up and down this trail plenty, usually on old Roanie. He feels choked up again. It don't seem right. There's no relief to getting closer to home this time. A cowboy oughtn't to leave his horse that way. If the Kid was down and hurt, he'd wager old Roanie would've stayed there beside him. He's getting cold again. He notices it, but it doesn't hurt. His back is exposed to the cold, which doesn't hurt, and to the big killer lion. That don't hurt either. That bloody lion comes down, and he'll get a big branch laid right between his bloody eyes. Kid walks on. He's too mad and too sorrowful to feel the cold.

Finally, Daddy stops at the salt trough and pulls the

extra saddle off Bludog. He is stashing it under the trough and telling the Kid that they'll ride double on in when Bludog raises his head and gives a nicker that is immediately answered not more than 200 yards away. They hear rocks rolling, then the sound of a big horse running free, then Roanie moves into sight out of the falling snow, head and tail high. He thunders right by them with a nicker, then turns and comes loping back, frisky as a colt.

Daddy and the Kid watch as he circles them, kicking up his heels. "Just look at that stumblin' son of a bitch prance now," says Daddy. He has a hint of a grin on his face. Finally, he takes the bridle out and catches Roanie, leading him over to the trough. Roanie is panting and sweaty, but his eyes are bright. Daddy saddles him, talking, seeming unmindful of the Kid. "Decided ya could git up off the ice after all, didja, you worthless rascal. It ain't hard to run across ice at all, is it? Not when yur savin' yore two-bit skin. Ha, we shoulda just tied you down there. Woulda been a nice lazy tender meal fur that cougar. Wished I had."

He is saddled, and Daddy flings up a rein. "Alright you old son of a bitch, you wanta run, you're gonna run." He swings into the saddle and cuts loose again with the wild cowboy yell, kicking Roanie into a high run. Him and Roanie disappear into the snowflakes toward the Burke Place. Kid and Bludog follow along at a more leisurely pace. Kid is warm now, and even though it is dark and snowing like blazes and he is tired, he feels pretty good, all considered.

As they drive home in the silence of the pickup, making new tracks in the snow, Daddy chuckles for no apparent reason a couple of times.

The Kid and Daddy eat supper alone, tersely answering Mother's questions with mostly "yes" and "no." Kid figures she's worried about him the whole day.

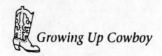

After supper he finds an old copy of the *Digest*. Beth is reading by coal oil light at the sewing table. "I gotta hand in a theme tomorrow," Kid tells her and throws down the *Digest*. "There's a dumb little story on page 42. It's somethin' about how not to bore people."

"I don't like to read junk like that," says Beth.

"Well, do me a favor. Change this around and kind of put it in my words so it don't seem copied."

"Shame on you. That's cheating. Anyway, if I use your words, you'll sure get an F."

"Aw, come on. I been workin' the whole day, so I ain't had time to think up anythin' to write about."

"If you'll stop saying *ain't*," says Beth, "maybe I'll do it."

"There's hardly a good word left that I dare say anymore," grumbles the Kid. And he tromps off to bed.

9

How Luna Kid
Busted the Old Cheater

W hen a little town rubs up against hard times, things begin to look not necessarily run-down, as in a city, but more like homemade.

Folks may have about as much to get by with during hard times, but less of it is "boughten." Whatever they use, live in, drive about, wear, is quite likely to reveal much of its owner's fallible craftsmanship. Cars may have wooden body parts. Clotheslines suspend quilts to dry, not blankets or sheets. Signs are hand-painted and shoes half-soled with glue. Everywhere one sees the copper rivet on pots and pans, tools, shoes, hats, gloves, even eyeglasses. In cemeteries the graves are marked with little iron plaques, die-stamped by hand. Gifts come wrapped in white tissue and may be simple wooden objects shaped with a coping saw or carved with a pocket knife. Greeting cards and valentines are most likely homely things, made out of cardboard and crepe paper. Even the kids look homemade with jeans faded to aborigine grey and typically double-

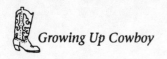

patched at the knee and rump, while their hand-me-down shirts, seams in disarray due to excess material, dangle like the skin of an old hog.

In good times, village people and their trappings take on a store-bought sheen, but in hard times everybody and everything begins to look, well, kind of organic. Such was the case in Luna, but with a prominent and noticeable exception. Old T.J. never stopped looking and acting homemade even during the good times. He never stopped making things by hand, either, and for the first fifty years of the century, he represented mister cottage industry of Luna Valley.

T.J. was a little shorter than average for those days and a little wider. He was also rather common in shoe size, but nothing else about the man was ordinary. His overall appearance, like his personality, was as counterpointed as a Wagnerian overture. Small, beady eyes peered out of a ruddy cherubic face, never bearded, but always appearing unshaven, cheeks shining pink through the grey whiskers. This cheerful countenance belied a voice usually gruff and feisty, aggressive, dogmatic, every bit as intimidating in tone as a pinscher's growl. At its cheerful best, though, that voice burst forth with a tone and cadence more like the bark of a terrier and sometimes with little more distinction between one sound and the next. T. J. was never one to use any great care in his choice of words. Whatever sounded right seemed right; thus, he generally expressed himself poetically but not precisely or very politely.

There's little evidence that T.J. ever drew a paycheck from anybody or made a dollar that wasn't already spent. But with hope and two strong hands, he made lots of other things: crates, furniture, caskets, toys, cedar chests, pallets, lamps, corral panels, all from wood sawed in his tiny sawmill, also homemade. But none of the above brought T.J. the identity that came with his skill in fashioning, from the rawest of materials, lightweight little pine panels that some people spoke of locally as T.J.'s wedges. Anyone who knew anything about roofs, though, considered them the best covering available, and T.J. gained wide recognition in those parts as the shingle-man of Luna Valley.

It's a wonder T.J. never got rich making and selling shingles. His were the straightest-grained, most split-resistant shingles known, and they outlasted any other roofing except for galvanized, which cost twice as much and made a whole house look tinny. He sold shingles just as fast as he could cut and bunch them. But everybody seemed to take for granted that T.J. wouldn't get rich off shingles or anything else. True, he was sober and active, and he had intimate knowledge of his product. But like most of his contemporaries, he carried through life an overload of impoverishing blemishes. One reason he never got rich off shingles was that he wouldn't make any until he absolutely had to have the money they would bring. And that usually happened only when his bills were so overdue that he couldn't show his face around three towns without getting dunned. This occurred with a frequency of only every second or third month. And, gosh, in between there was other stuff to make, tinkering to do, things needing fixing, etcetera.

Another reason T.J. seemed destined never to be rich (except for a few hours those four or five days a year when he delivered shingles) was perhaps related to an unbearable abrasiveness, which also may explain why he couldn't, or wouldn't, work for hire. Couple these problems with his well-deserved reputation for being slow to pay help, if he paid at all, and one can see that T.J. had little future as a manufacturing entrepreneur. He raised a family of strong, bright, handsome, redheaded boys. By all appearances, they left as soon as they could. He hired itinerants and drove most of them clean out of town with his argumen-

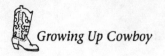

tative and aggressive behavior. (This usually happened just before the first payday.) He brought in relatives. They soon left in a name-calling huff.

Regardless of how tough the times, anybody could always get a job at T.J.'s, simply because nobody looking for a job was fool enough to work there. Nobody, that is, except the Luna Kid, who found himself, one fine July day, needing some cash to buy a fishing license. . . .

* * * * *

The Kid steps up on a block to peer inside the big vat. It's square, like a cake pan, and smells powerfully and sweetly of saturated pinewood. T.J. is standing there barefoot in about six inches of water. His soiled bib overalls are rolled up to his knees. He's been spreading chunks of split pine, each about a quarter of a trunk section in size and maybe a foot and a half long. They cover the floor of the vat.

"Which one are you?" he asks.

He nods, satisfied with the Kid's answer. "I figgered you wuz the younger one." He stares then. "Them glasses is too big fur yur face. Make you look like a fool."

The Kid fidgets. He's sensitive about his spectacles because everybody seems to think they are too fancy for Luna. "I come to see if you needed a shingle buncher," he says.

"I'll pay ya fifteen cents a bunch," snaps T.J. "Now git that bucket 'n start dippin' while the ditch is runnin' full."

The Kid remembers hearing townsfolk accuse T.J. of stealing reservoir water that belongs on down the ditch. It's caused some hard feelings. Rather furtively, he dips the five-gallon can half-full and hands it up. T.J. dumps the water and passes the bucket down for a refill. After at least an hour of this, the Kid is tired and has a question.

"How much you pay when I ain't bunchin'?"

"Thirty-five cents an hour," T.J. answers. "That's the goin' rate fur kids." He pulls out an old railroad watch. "Les see. It's jist now 2:30."

Kid glances at the sun. He knows for sure it can't be a minute past two o'clock. And he's worked at least an hour already. The Kid doesn't say anything, just keeps dipping. The water head in the ditch is sinking. Kid can get only a quarter-bucketful now. T.J. curses at finding mud in the bucket.

"Them bastards up ditch have turned the water," he growls. "Well, I reckon we got enough anyhow."

He pulls the watch again and holds it out for the Kid to see. "Looky here. It's 3:30. You've done put in an hour." He takes out his pencil and makes a mark on one of the rough pine planks that frame the entry to the shingle mill. "Ever time you git five marks we'll draw an X thru 'em. That'll mean I owe yu a dollar seventy. And ever time you do one bunch you kin mark a slash below there. When you git five slashes I owe ya seventy cents. Now go roll them old tires from under the shed until I git a fire goin'."

T. J. builds a pitch pine fire at either end of the vat, then motions to the Kid to throw on the tires. They burn with an angry black smoke and terrific heat. He stands back and looks at the Kid. "You git home now. Come back after dark and put some more tires on, an' tomorrow all day you feed the fire. We'll start cuttin' the day after."

The Kid stands there looking down, kicking the dirt with a worn tennis shoe. "I been wondering," he finally says, "how come if you pay me thirty-five cents an hour, I only git a dollar seventy for five hours. And if you pay fifteen cents a bunch, how come I only git seventy cents for five."

T. J. is surprised. He stares at the Kid derisively. "Why hell's fire, that ain't no big deal. I jist rounded them

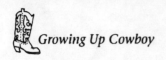

numbers off to do away with the five's and make it easier to figger. It's nothin' but a few pennies."

The Luna Kid thinks a while, still kicking gently at the dirt. Finally he looks up, but away from T.J. "Oh sure," he nods. "I see now why you done it."

The Kid knows that T.J. has lots of tricks in his bag, but this is a new one. He's dog-tired and there's a blister beginning to swell on his hand from lifting the big can. "Long as it's only a few cents and don't really matter, I'll just take eighty cents for five bunches and a dollar eighty for five hours. That'll be even easier to figger 'cause it's all in even numbers."

T.J. stares at the Luna Kid. It's the first time he's really looked at him beyond the plastic-rimmed specs. He seems startled and surprised. Finally he says, "Oh well now, hells bells, if ya think I'm tryin' to cheat, we'll jist go ahead and do the figgerin' in five's."

The Kid's dander is getting up. He's disgusted with T.J. And he's beginning to feel sort of noble, now, like he's carrying on the cause of humanity. "Lemmie take your pencil," he says.

T.J. looks puzzled, but he reaches out his flat carpenter's pencil. Kid snatches it, quickly puts another mark alongside the first one on the plank, and hands the pencil back to T.J. "That'll be okay with me," he says, and heads home across the field.

He is surprised that T.J. hadn't raised any objection, instead just looked at him in an interested way, maybe even a little respectful, for the first time. But it worries the Kid, too. The old codger gave in awful easy. Kid will have to look out and keep on his toes all the time.

* * * * *

It's early morning and Kid can hear the crash . . . crash
. . . crash of T.J.'s shingle mill running. The shingle knife,
suggestive of a guillotine, is regulated by a rod attached to the
rim of a big cast-iron wheel. Every revolution of the wheel
pushes the guillotine up, then draws it crashing down again.
The sound is coming in perfect timing: bang . . . bang . . . bang.
. . . Then suddenly there comes a ca-whoosh . . . ca-whoosh
. . . bang . . . bang . . . ca-whoosh . . . bang . . . bang . . . bang
. . . ca-whoosh . . . ca-whoosh . . . bang . . . bang. . . . T. J. is
starting to feed the hot wooden blocks sideways against the
plunging knife. And then the racket smoothes out to a
cadence of a ca-whooshes. The banging starts again while T.J.
fishes another steaming block from the vat. More ca-whooshes
and more banging, then more ca-whooshes, and the Kid
knows there's getting to be a pile of hot shingles under the
guillotine. He'd better get going.

Inside the plank shack that houses the mill, he
watches T.J. standing there on the platform feeding the
guillotine. It's tricky work and frightfully dangerous to
keep pressing a slippery hot wooden block against the
steel bars that stand the width of a shingle behind the
knife. One slip of either hand and—the Kid doesn't even
dare think about it. They'd never get him within ten feet
of that guillotine, and here T.J.'s fingers keep pushing,
pushing, until they're only three chops away. Kid watches
with fascination and horror as those living fingers edge
ever closer to the awful hammering knife, then fall away
only to start pressing forward again with the next steaming block. He shudders. What if the dreadful cadence of
the operation kind of hypnotizes T.J. and he just keeps
pushing forward until. . . . Kid takes a deep breath, but
quietly. He sure doesn't want to startle T.J. He turns to the
box where he labors.

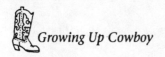

Bunching shingles in those days involved trimming the edges of each shingle and gathering perhaps seventy-five of them into a neat, compact, tightly wired bundle. This was done in a box or mold into which the buncher laid shingles one at a time. Skills required were scarcely more intricate than tying a double bowknot in a shoe lace and no more interesting. It could have been an awful bore. And it was indeed a bore when T.J. chopped shingles, or was otherwise engaged, leaving the Kid to bunch alone.

But generally T.J. joined the Kid at bunching. He was a whiz at it. He and the Kid sat there back-to-back, maybe ten feet apart, bunching and talking. T.J. was lonely, and given an audience, his mouth could move as fast as his hands. But T.J. and the Kid were a generation apart. They hardly talked the same language. Soon conversation paled. So they stopped talking and began arguing. That never paled.

Maybe it was boredom that drove T.J. and the Kid to argumentation or perhaps raw, reactive elements within the chemistry of each body. It seemed as if the Good Lord had put two chattering jays into a cage who were destined never to agree with one another. Their arguments were spontaneous, irrational, often viciously personal and abusive; therefore, they were endless, due to eventual breakdown of logic and decorum.

Within days, the Kid and T.J. had settled into a routine: T.J. provokes debate with outrageous statement. The Kid challenges substance of the contention. T.J. verbally attacks the Kid for stupidity. The Kid counters with slashing assault on state of the mental condition that propounded such nonsense. T.J. striking back, voice louder, defends with wild, irrelevant logic. Kid, voice steadier, stabs at his opponent, sometimes sarcastically. T.J., in a name-calling frenzy, berates the Kid for failings and flaws ranging from physical to character and mental states both conscious and unconscious.

Their fierce and noisy banter would rage on until the shingles were bunched and T.J. would sigh, pull on his canvas gloves, crank the rusty old International engine, fish out a block with his tongs, and begin cutting again. The debate remained unresolved, but with each new batch of shingles, there was something new to argue about.

The ritual would be repeated time and again—T.J., seemingly born with a yen for lighthearted abusive dialogue, who couldn't carry on with just anybody (especially his sons), vs. the Luna Kid, with his penchant for theatrical sassing and comic cerebral sparring (and a father who'd put up with neither). They came together in the weather-beaten mill shed and argued and sassed and sparred endlessly as the flies buzzed out the long, hot afternoons, and the stacks of bunched shingles, merely a by-product of verbal gymnastics, grew ever higher, and the slashes and X's on the door frame multiplied.

It wasn't long until word got around that the best show in town was T.J. and the Kid arguing. Sometimes they'd draw a snickering audience. Generally, whoever it was never stayed around, though, because this brand of abrasive argument proved endlessly entertaining only to the participants.

One day, in a rare serious vein, the Kid asked T.J., "When you gonna pay me for all the tallies on the door frame?"

"When I sell them shingles."

"Well, for now I need a fishin' license. Thought maybe I could collect that much today."

T.J. opened his wallet. "How much fur a license?"

"Three bucks."

"Hell, I got seven. We'll both go. I ain't been fishin' in forty years."

T.J. and the Luna Kid squat on the dam that creates Hamblin Lake. T.J. has a bamboo pole with a cork float.

Kid can see T.J.'s baited hook dangling in the transparent water about ten feet from shore. The Kid's own worm is farther out, resting on red stones on the bottom. The little roundish lake is about a hundred yards from end to end. There are some tourists from Phoenix at the other side. Closer by, the Kid recognizes old man Rothlesberger of Alpine. He is baiting the hook of a fat lady visitor from Clifton. Except for the three groups, the lake is deserted.

The Kid sees a small trout eyeing T.J.'s hook from only a half-inch distance. It circles away, then comes back to be joined by a bigger one, both toying with the worm.

"Better look out. You got a fish there," warns the Kid. T.J. excitedly grabs his pole, jerking the line and hook clean out of the water and into the branches of an aspen tree behind him.

"Damn you," growls T.J. at the Kid. "Where's the fish?"

"Well, you jerked before he bit. That wasn't too smart."

"You dirty whelp. You told me to."

Old man Rothlesberger and the fat lady are snickering. The Kid's pole wiggles then. He grabs it and gives a little line. It tightens again. The Kid jerks it up and reels in fast. He pulls a flopping, colorful cutthroat trout up onto the bank. It's maybe eight inches long.

T.J. dances about in excitement. "Damn you, you hound, that's my fish."

Old man Rothlesberger and the fat lady are laughing aloud now, egging on T.J. and the kid, and the tourists from Phoenix are looking their way.

The Kid holds the trout out to taunt T.J. "See, you catch fish in water, not trees."

"You rotten-ass whelp," T.J. mutters. "Gimme that fish. I had 'im first."

The Kid smirks, sinks a gunny sack at the water's edge and puts the fish, still flopping, inside. "Better git your bait out of the tree. We ain't here to catch birds."

By the time T.J. gets himself untangled, the Kid has another trout. T.J. is baiting his hook again when old man Rothlesberger sings out, "Ain't you fellers from Luna?"

"Yeah," says T.J. "Name's Halson. Grew up in Nutri."

"Oh shore," says old man Rothlesberger. "There was a batch of you Halsons. Which is you?"

"I'm the one married the big Hendricks girl out uv Alpine."

Old man Rothlesberger nods and turns back to his fish pole.

Kid is thinking it's sort of unkind to mention big girls in front of the fat lady, but he agrees in his mind there's not a better way of describing T.J.'s wife. She's a honey-can wider than T.J. and some taller.

The Kid brings in another flopping trout. T.J. glowers at him.

"Put your hook deeper," says the Kid, "and maybe you'll git one."

"Oh piss," says T.J. " I wouldn't bend my back fur one a them little bitty things." About then his cork goes under and T.J. jerks up with a mighty grunt. Out flies a little trout, barely a keeper. T.J. hops around trying to pick it up. Finally he gets his hands on it. His cheeks have brightened from pastel pink to cherry red under the grey stubble. He holds the trout out toward old man Rothlesberger and the fat lady. They clap. One of the Phoenix tourists gives a whistle from across the lake.

T.J. tosses the trout in the Kid's gunny sack and shouts excitedly so all can hear, "We got four now." He quickly catches two more and, eyes glowing, tells the Kid, "Git off yur lazy butt and put a float on. You might catch a fish."

"I'm awful glad," says the Kid, "that you've quit chasin' them tiny things away from your hook to mine. I'm fixin' to git a big one."

They sit quietly for a moment. Then T.J. pipes up, "I

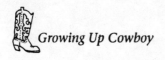

reckon the best time to catch a big fish is in the rain."

Old man Rothlesberger eyes him with some derision. "Well now," he says, "there ain't no better reason for a big one to git hungry in the rain than for a little one to."

"Shore there's a reason," insists T.J. "Rain on water jist the same thing to a fish as wind is to you. Now, don't you git lots hungrier on a windy day?"

The Kid sees an opportunity. "That only happens if you're a windbag," he drawls.

Old man Rothlesberger and the fat lady let loose a guffaw.

"That kid a yourn," says old man Rothlesberger, "he's some blade. Heh, heh."

"Ha," retorts T.J. "He ain't nothin' to me but a damned lazy poo——." Just then his float begins to quiver. "Poo——, poo——." He jerks excitedly on the bamboo pole. "Po——o——t." And he grabs on the bank for the flopping trout. "Yeah," he says breathlessly, "jist a damned lazy hound."

Old man Rothlesberger, the fat lady, and the Luna Kid are all laughing at T.J.'s antics.

"I reckon," says the old man, "you meant to say pooch hound."

"I meant what I said," barks T.J., somewhat cheerfully, throwing the trout in the sack.

"You called that poor boy a Poot Hound," charges the fat lady in a demure, shaming voice, but ending with a giggle.

"Well, that's jist exactly what I meant," intones T.J., flipping his bait back into the water. "Shore he's a Poot Hound. Jist a damned lazy Poot Hound."

The Kid grits his teeth. Such things have a way of getting around. The Kid well knows that old man Rothlesberger is father-in-law to Orvil R., who lives in Luna. Orvil has a wagging tongue, too. And, cuss the luck and T.J.'s runny mouth, "poot" is the word used by mothers and girls as a genteel substitute for "fart."

Kid remembers sitting on the stage at school just last winter. He was all relaxed except for an anal contraction holding in a build-up of bean gas. Sue Ellen and Vera sneaked up from behind the curtains and gave him a surprise shove that brought forth, instead of the expected grasping at the stage, a noisy, ragged release. Worst of all was the shocked silence following the fart. Finally, a rich, acrid smell wafted up around the Kid's nostrils, and the mortified girls took silent leave to creep back behind the curtains. Later he heard hysterical giggles and staccato whispers from there and knew word of the incident was getting around.

And now T.J.'s "Poot Hound." Kid's neck is feeling flushed and hot. Maybe it won't get around. Anyway, he'll make T.J. pay for it. "Why do big fish git any hungrier when it rains than little fish?" he asks.

"Cause when it rains the sun don't shine, and that makes big fish hungry."

"Well, if all sizes of people git hungry when the wind blows, how come only big fish git hungry when the sun don't shine?"

T. J. glares darkly at the Kid, who he knows is trying to tangle him. He doesn't like that, not with an audience.

"Well, fish ain't the same as people, you scabhead."

"Jist a while ago, you said rain on fish was like wind on people. Now git your story straight."

T.J. thinks for a while. A breeze riffles the water and sets the aspen leaves to rustling. The Arizona sky is cloudless above them and deep blue. In the lovely warm afternoon, only the sounds of the breeze and forest come into the ear. Finally, T.J. says, "The difference is in the electricity."

Kid looks at him, on guard.

"Yeah, electricity," repeats T.J. "Ya see, we can't catch big fish because they don't bite when it don't rain. And it

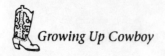

don't rain 'cause we're taking all the electricity out a the air to light houses."

The Luna Kid throws up his hands in mock exasperation. "What's that got to do with rain?"

"Well, even a lazy Poot Hound ought to see that now they're runnin' generators in all the towns around, and then all the cars and trucks are takin' electricity out a the air to charge their batteries. There ain't enough left fur lightnin'. So it can't rain."

"Lord a mighty," says Luna Kid, "that's some cockwhollopin' excuse for catchin' little tiny fish."

Just then the fat lady screams. They hear a thudding splash, and she screams again. Old man Rothlesberger yells "Look out," and there's another mighty splash. The fat lady has hooked a big rainbow. She winds him in a few turns, squealing, then the fish pulls back and starts a run. The fat lady whoops so loud she can't hear old man Rothlesberger yelling instructions. T.J. drops his bamboo pole and lopes gingerly over to stand beside the fat lady. It's a scene the Kid won't soon forget: T.J. and old man Rothlesberger standing in bib overalls, one to each side of the fat lady, framing her and her bobbing breasts. The big square tail of the trout beats the water in front of them. Then the three are dragging the wallowing fish up the bank halfway out of the water, but suddenly there's a bloodcurdling scream from the fat lady. Her trophy has flopped off the hook and back into the water. A loud splash follows another scream as old man Rothlesberger plunges his thick body into the water to form a human fence between the lake and the trout, and there's yet another scream and another splash as the powerful trout flips out of his grasp and T.J. sacrificially hurls himself into the melee. T.J. and old man Rothlesberger are threshing, splashing, sputtering, and shouting. The fat lady screams. The trout leaps, flops, and darts. Suddenly T.J. has him pinned between two arms and his whiskery chin. Then he comes wading out on his knees, soaked and muddy, grinning triumphantly, old man Rothlesberger right behind, the fat lady still screaming and jumping.

T.J. lays the exhausted trout on safe ground. There's a hush as the three stand, dripping and panting, looking down at the fish. Kid knows the big rainbow will weigh five pounds or more. He's never seen such a fish. The tourists from Phoenix are buzzing.

T.J.'s float begins to move again, and the Kid calls out to him. He runs back to his pole, soaking wet, stubby legs churning, excitement sparking his grey eyes. Kid can't remember seeing T.J. run before. T.J. pulls in another small trout.

Kid is silent for a while, letting the commotion die down. "Well," the Kid says finally, "maybe the best time to catch big fish is when the sun's beatin' down."

"Shore it is," says T.J., still somewhat breathless. "You saw what she jist done, didn't ya? And ain't the sun shinin'?"

"Well, jist a minute ago, you was sayin' . . . "

"I wasn't sayin' any damn sich thing," T.J. interrupts the Kid. "You got ears so dirty your pa could plant taters there. You can't hear nothin' straight."

Old man Rothlesberger and the fat lady have secured the rainbow and settled back. They are paying attention. The Phoenix tourists are staring toward T.J. and the Kid.

"What about all that electricity stuff? You the same as said just now that we'd catch bigger fish if they'd quit takin' electricity out of the air."

"Hell, Kid. You don't even know what electricity is. Go ahead, yur so smart. What is it?"

"Sure I know. But you brought it up. You tell me."

"It's the same as lightnin', you peckerhead."

"Then how come it don't flash and thunder?"

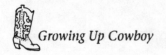

"If I explained, you wouldn't understand a word. Yur too dumb. Anyway, there ain't nothin' a damned lazy Poot Hound, who's jist barely smart enough to bunch shingles, needs to know about electricity." He turns then to old man Rothlesberger and the fat lady, "Ain't that right, folks?"

They give a hooting cheer in unison. And from across the lake, Kid hears clapping by the Phoenix tourists. He hunkers down next to his pole. In his dealings with T.J. he has developed a certain obstinacy he never had before. All the same, the Kid knows when he's whipped.

Early next morning, the Kid is walking toward the shingle mill and hears a yell. He turns to see a grinning Mendis Butler, who calls out loudly, "Hey, how you doin', you lazy old . . . heh, heh, heh. . . ." Mendis pauses, and the grin widens to show his pearly white upper plate, "Poot Hound . . . heh, heh, heh."

Orvil has made the rounds already and done his work well. A whole new appellation, or call it a cross, has been laid on the perhaps deserving shoulders of the sassy Luna Kid. He will reluctantly bear it the rest of his juvenile life.

* * * * *

It's early in the morning of the last Wednesday before school starts. The Luna Kid is excited, not just because him and T.J. are taking the old truck to Springerville, but because they're hauling the shingles, so it'll be payday at last. He's counted the X's and slashes on the mill door frame and done his multiplication. Adding in the extras he's put there to kind of offset T.J.'s self-serving way of keeping time and subtracting the three dollars for the fishing license, the Kid has twenty-seven dollars coming.

They gas up at the station, but only after T.J. assures, "I'm gonna pay my bill jist as soon we git back from deliverin' these shingles."

T.J. lets the Kid drive the old truck, instructing him gently along the way. Kid wonders at that. Old T.J.'s own boys allegedly taught each other to drive because their pa was so impatient and cranky. Once or twice along the way the Kid tries to get T.J. into an argument but nothing doing. T.J. doesn't want to argue today. He talks incessantly along the way, though, tells some jokes and anecdotes about his own boyhood, asks the Kid questions about school and all. Once, when the Kid mentions that he's planning to buy a new pair of boots, T.J. shifts the subject back to driving and trucks, which he knows will interest the Kid.

They pull up at the General "Merc." The Kid knows that's where T.J. delivers shingles and buys groceries. T.J. goes in the store, and the manager follows him out, looks over the shingles, and nods. "Okay," he tells T.J. "Now let's see, yur bill is. . . . " T.J. hushes him suddenly, turns to the Kid, takes out his wallet. There's a single dollar bill inside. He gives it to the Kid. "Go git yurself a haircut," he says. The Kid finds a barbershop where the sign reads seventy-five cents. The sly barber takes him to a cleaning via a shampoo and special Wildroot treatment on top of the haircut. The bill is a dollar thirty-five.

"I'll go find this feller who owes me money and come back," promises the blushing Kid.

He sees T.J. on the sidewalk in front of Becker's store. He is with two men the Kid has seen before. He thinks they are T.J.'s relatives. The three of them listen with some levity to the Kid's problem. T.J. gives him a fifty-cent piece.

Kid is disappointed. He'd expected twenty-three dollars. As he turns away, T.J. asks one of the men, "We free and clear now?" The man grunts.

On the way home, T.J. doesn't say much, and neither does the Kid, who's a little stung that he never got paid in

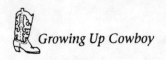

Springerville where he could have spent the money, instead of in Luna where he can't.

Back in Luna, they stop at the service station. T.J. goes inside. The Kid hears some discussion in there, and pretty soon T.J. comes out. He doesn't look too happy or bother to say goodbye.

T.J. knows what's on the Kid's mind when he drops him off. "Come over tomorrow. We'll count the tallies 'n settle up," he says. The Kid nods, but he is apprehensive. At one time or another just about everybody who's dealt with T.J. has come up on the short end of the stick. On the other hand, old T.J. has just sold, by his own admission, the biggest batch of shingles ever. More than two hundred dollars worth.

Early in the morning, the Luna Kid walks across the alfalfa field, wet with dew, to T.J.'s place. He waits at the shed by the tallies for T.J. to show. He hasn't intended to check the tallies 'cause he knows them by heart. But then a yellow streak on the door frame draws his eye. It hadn't looked that way before. His throat tightens as he leans closer and sees that a strip of bark has peeled right off the edge of the board. More than half of his tallies had been scrawled on that strip. Desperately the Kid looks around for the bark. It is nowhere to be found. He counts the remaining tallies. All total, there are only six slashes and three X's. Well, the Kid won't tell T.J. about the missing tallies. He knows the number, no question about it.

He hears a door slam. T.J. comes hurrying toward him. He seems angry or distraught. Some people claim T.J. always looks mean. Well, this morning he does look mean. His voice is clipped with the Doberman bark that Kid has noted he often uses on people he doesn't like. Without so much as "hi" or "howdy" he says, "You see what yore owed. I got the money right here."

Suddenly the Kid realizes what is happening. He's on

to T.J. and not happy, not a bit. He shouts at the advancing figure. "These tallies ain't right. I had more of 'em on a strip of bark that got peeled off."

T.J. doesn't look at him but at a paper in his hand. His voice is cold and unfriendly. "Twelve slashes and three X's adds up to fourteen and a quarter. I done paid you four and a half. You got nine seventy-five comin'."

The Kid is furious. "I won't take a penny 'til you pay what I really got comin'. That's twenty-four dollars in all."

"Here's a ten dollar bill," says T.J. "It's a little somethin' extree. Take this and git out a here."

Kid notices then that T.J.'s freckled old hand, the one holding the bill, is shaking. He's still looking away, but his wallet is open. There's nothing left inside. Almost in a daze, the Kid takes the bill and stuffs it in his pocket. He swallows and starts to say something about a mistake, but T.J. cuts him off. "I said fur you to git on home. I got plenty to do."

The Kid takes off across the alfalfa patch. Every second step he can feel the crumpled ten dollar bill pressing against his thigh. He's lucky. It's the last ten dollars from all those shingles, and he has it, T.J. don't.

He feels numb all over except for where the bill presses against his leg and a sensation of sound from out of the past, a beat against his ear with the cadence of his own heart, ca-whoosh ... ca-whoosh ... ca-whoosh ... ca-whoosh, as T.J.'s strong, stubby fingers press ever closer to the hammering guillotine. Is it fair? Those hands at risk should hold the last ten dollars. T.J. has a new line of credit now, but, oh, those shingles have made him a slave. Every one he drops is spent before it hits the ground. Next year the Kid'll keep a tally on paper in his own pocket. When he announces that, it'll cause a dandy argument and some fun all around, lots better than now. No good seeing T.J. humbled and ashamed.

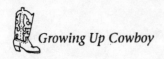

Kid kills a couple of hours and gets home in time for dinner. "Well," asks Mother, "did T.J. pay what he owes you?" There's an edge of doubt in her voice.

"Shore did," answers the Kid. "And he gave me somethin' extra."

"Well, I declare," says Mother.

* * * * *

Years later, as rookie editor of a magazine, the Kid finds himself face to face with a tough, seasoned ad executive who competes for page space and loves fighting duels with words at eighty decibels. Of ruddy complexion and beady twinkling eyes, this thundering adversary has a way of overwhelming opposition with threatening voice and domineering, sometimes subversive, personality. Even though he is thought to possess a humane and gentle heart, almost nobody can withstand his intimidating onslaughts.

The Luna Kid is ready.

10

Cave Man
in Residence

As you've learned, the Mogollon Breaks is a sparsely settled land. But it was not always so. A thousand years ago, the quiet pristine draws, mesas, canyons, and streams of the Blue and San Francisco valleys nurtured far more people than they do today.

These were peaceful Indians, who built pit houses of poles and stone along shallow streams that poured flood waters out over fields of corn, squash, and beans. These Indians, of the so-called Mogollon Culture, seemed to prefer sites of about 6,000–7,500 feet, where oak and mahogany mingled with piñon and juniper, but towering ponderosas commanded the skyline. They also loved high vistas. Thus they gravitated in large numbers to the Mogollon Breaks. They occupied these lands for some 800 years, then departed for parts unknown long before the coming of the Spaniards. They left behind much that they had made from the earth itself: their dwellings, art, weapons, tools, and pottery. This is a land, then, that is deeply

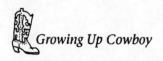

imprinted and ever haunted by a tenant of ages past.

The culture spilled beyond the Mogollon Breaks into the Gila, with its cozy cliff dwellings, and southward into the Mimbres Valley, where Mogollon people decorated their pots with some of the most daring and startling images ever seen in the New World.

Others of the Mogollon Culture crossed high ridges to the west, into lands of the Little Colorado River. Here some of them found a new kind of dwelling, like no other, perhaps, in the history of human habitation. These "apartments" lay along the great basaltic mesas that are so plentiful in higher country of the Little Colorado. Basalt is a tough, heavy lava that refuses to bend. When stressed, it breaks into jillions of irregular blocks, some as big as a house. Imagine the pile of boulders when a mountainside splits and falls away. Sometimes it's ten stories high. And within this jumble are thousands of cavities varying in size from as big as a master bedroom to as tiny as a bookcase.

For centuries, Indians occupied these cavities. From all appearances they lived, loved, multiplied, and died there. They made and decorated their earthy pottery, wove their baskets, polished their arrows, chipped masterful arrowheads out of obsidian, ground and strung beads of bone and turquoise, and cast fetishes of clay. It must have been a rather uncomfortable, yet serene, secure place of abode. No enemy would dare to enter such a fortress of boulders, where corridors were as wildly irregular as July sunsets, and where intruders could be entombed forever through the expedient of rolling a rock across an opening. . . .

* * * * *

It is a raw and wintry day, but Jimmy and the Kid are warm as laid eggs here on the rocks. There's something about this place that seems to trap and hold heat. Maybe that's why the Indians liked it so much. Kid is seated on the edge of one of the biggest boulders he has ever seen. It is a faded red in color. Below his dangling feet there's nothing but air. Slip off, and they would find only a grease spot down below. Kid is a little apprehensive sitting here, but Jimmy sat first, and he's not about to let Jimmy get another dare up on him.

All morning, Kid and Jimmy have been peering down through rocky openings into shadowy cavities below. If they can see a floor, and it's not too dark, Kid crawls inside for a look. If they can't see a floor, they drop in a rock and listen. If the hole is not too deep but dark, Kid says, "I reckon there's nothing there." Jimmy knows that's the signal for him to crawl in and check it out because the Kid won't. For his part, the Kid figures that Jimmy can risk his own neck any way he wants to. Kid is pretty sure that Jimmy didn't hear about Albert Skousen, who told last winter of finding a whole nest of hibernating rattlesnakes over in the malpais caves above Nutrioso Creek. He claimed the snakes had gathered themselves into a ball two or three times bigger than a basketball. He shot into that ball, and snakes flew in every direction. Old Albert, he got the hell out of there in a hurry.

Things are going good here. No need to risk getting Jimmy spooked. Him and the Kid have found a batch of worked flint, several broken points, and lots of pottery shards. So Kid is not about to tell Jimmy about those snakes. Old-timers used to find whole pots in the caves. Of course, that was years ago. Nobody in Nutrioso could remember the last pot found here. They all said it was a waste of time looking, because the caves have been scoured for years by everybody with enough wind and legs to climb up there. Kid knew not many folks were so equipped. That's why he figured it was well worth a look.

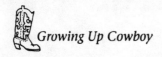

They don't talk much as they eat their lunch here on the edge of the cliff, concentrating on the view. A thousand or so feet below, and about a mile to the east they can see the little school at Nutrioso where Kid's mother has a one-year contract to teach all eight grades. Beyond is a scattering of houses and a sawmill. That's about all there is to Nutrioso, but you get a heck of a view of the Arizona side of Escudilla Mountain from here. It rears so steep and high above Nutri road that it makes the place look even more insignificant, like the toy towns you order from Sears and Roebuck.

Kid wonders if the Indians wouldn't have sat here on a winter day, feeling the warmth of the rocks on their haunches. They would stare down at the creek with its icy edges and browned-off meadows, or they might study Escudilla Mountain for sign of gods or devils. The old Indians either revered or feared this mountain. Kid knows that, because right on top, near the Forest Service lookout, is a spring where you can find the most beautiful beads and arrowheads you ever saw—so painstaking and perfect that you couldn't imagine a use or need for them other than to appease or praise some kind of god.

Jimmy has finished his lunch and begins to fidget on the rock. He's getting a little tired of this, Kid knows. He'll be wanting to head back soon. Kid's gentle, easygoing friend has a girl now, and he's not as patient as he used to be. Kid is deeply fond of Jimmy. They took instantly to one another when Kid moved here from Luna. Jimmy is as close as any friend you could have, and, of course, if he should get bitten by a hibernating rattler, which is sure unlikely, Kid would come to his aid. A ball of snakes, that might be different, though. You might have to sacrifice even your best friend to a whole ball of those devils.

At the start of the school year, Kid and Jimmy used to walk along the school corridors and the sidewalk out front with an arm around one another. It didn't mean anything except "we're buddies." About midterm some slick kids moved from California to Round Valley High School. They laughed at Kid and Jimmy. "What are you," they asked, "a couple of queers?" After the friends learned what queers meant, the arm business ended quickly.

Jimmy would love to find a pot, but other than that he's not much interested in these Indians. Kid has a collection of arrowheads, beads, and flint knives. He has fragments of tomahawks and a clay fetish that looks somewhat like an antelope. He found these things while crawling around on ruins or near springs. It is exciting to find something so old lying there untarnished in the sun. Kid thinks of it as a handwritten message that says "hello" from a thousand years past.

Kid says nothing of this to Jimmy. All Jimmy wants is a pot, and he's about ready to quit. He's talking about checking Coulter Creek to see how the fishing is. Kid will have to crawl into those dark caves by himself this afternoon or leave them be.

At about midafternoon, Kid is searching alone. He's gotten a little bolder now, after sneaking into dozens of caves and seeing nary a snake ball. Besides, these caves all seem to have a definite tilt to the west; so the light is better this time of day. He squeezes into an opening that seemed at first to be just a blank wall. That's because a rock shelf juts out enough to hide a break in the rocks about a bushel basket in size. That shelf is all the Kid can remember later about the cave, except that it is lighter inside than he expected, due to a split in the rock ceiling that lets in a beam of sunlight.

Kid takes a deep breath, as his eyes adjust, and expels it instantly because there they are, nearly close enough to touch. And all he can do with what little breath is left in his body is tilt toward the rocky skylight and scream for Jimmy.

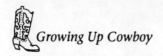

It is a scene that will etch deeply into the memory of the Luna Kid, deeper than any other of his lifetime. The two pots are far bigger than any he has ever seen or imagined. One is lying on its side, its dull, smooth neck facing him. The other pot stands upright, directly under the beam of light that casts uneven shadows along its textured neck. Both bottoms are jaggedly broken. Beyond that, the huge pots are as perfectly symmetrical as the day they were shaped, a thousand, eleven, twelve hundred years past . . . maybe more.

All the Kid and Jimmy can do in the confines of the dim cave is to jump up and down, hugging each other, yelling all the cuss words and other expletives they know. It's the first time they've hugged since those Californians came to Round Valley.

Traffic stops in Nutrioso, even Highway 260 traffic, as Luna Kid and Jimmy come beaming down the road, lugging two great pots ten centuries old.

Thus begins the legend of Round Valley's teenage cave man. It is an identity neither sought nor cultivated by the Luna Kid. But once you have momentum, it is hard to stop, as we shall see.

(Months afterward, by official request, Kid guides a hearty University of Arizona archeology professor into the labyrinth of caves above Coulter Creek. They find pottery shards and flint chips in many caves and in one a well-worn metate. In yet another cave, they come upon an angry, coiled rattler. The good professor goes away interested but a little shaken. As far as the Kid knows, he never comes back.)

* * * * *

Some people rave about the beautiful hills and mesas that encircle Round Valley. Kid's eyes see only those long

110

double rims of rock that telegraph a split on the hillside and possible caves below. Kid has played hooky twice in the last three weeks to check out caves. He might have ditched more, but it's hard to get a ride out to the mesas where the caves are.

That's no problem today. Pervis and his Model A are ditching, too. Pervis has never been to the caves, and he doesn't know anything about Indians. Strangely, though, he looks the part of a true cave man, with heavy brows, long arms, and a squat build. He's not the best-looking guy in school, but Pervis has one thing all the guys envy: a Model A coupe with a rumble seat. Pervis is popular with girls because they love that rumble seat.

Pervis is waiting when Luna Kid arrives on the Nutrioso bus. They sneak off easily without being seen. At the cattle guard on the mesa road, they meet Hank Cosper, who owns the ranch closest to the caves. Pervis knows him. "Is it okay if we look for arrowheads out here?" asks Pervis.

"Why ain't you boys in school?"

"Aw . . . we got our work done, and they gave us a day off."

Cosper grins. He doesn't believe it, but there's not much mischief in hunting arrowheads. "Okay, but tomorrow you git back in school."

By noon they haven't found much. Pervis allows he'll go home for lunch and then come back for an afternoon of exploring. Kid has brought his lunch. He's just finished eating when the Model A comes honking down the lane, kicking up dust. Three girls are packed in the cab beside Pervis, and two more are in the rumble seat. "I swung by the school and picked 'em up," says Pervis exultantly. "A bunch more are comin'."

The girls are giddy with the daring of ditching school together. "How you doin', Cave Man?" They paw at the Kid. "So this is where you been hangin' out."

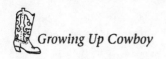

Kid is shy with the girls. But when he can get Pervis to one side, he lays into him. "You bloomin' idiot. Now we're in lotsa trouble."

"Don't worry, they ain't about to expel us all. Looky who else is here." A line of cars comes down the lane. There's a pickup in the caravan, its box lined with noisy kids, howling and singing.

Kid doesn't know what to do. He has a girl on each arm. They giggle and carry on. They want to see the caves. As others come up, they're giving him the business about helping find a pot or getting lost all together in the dark, hee . . . hee. Finally, about half the kids follow him into the caves. No telling what happened to the rest.

An hour or so later he is pointing to smoke stains at the opening of a cavity and giving a little lecture to Sue and June about the Indians. Pervis has disappeared, but now he yells down at the Kid. "You better git up here quick. Vera and Lana have broke into old man Cosper's house."

Kid hurries down the slope toward the picnic table where a bunch of students are milling around. Pervis comes running to meet him. "They broke a window and stole a carton of Luckies. They got some cookies, too, and a big ham," he says.

Kid loses his composure. "Hey, you guys gotta take all that stuff back," he screams. "Old Cosper knows me and Pervis are out here. We'll be in for it."

June is offering a pack of cigarettes around. "They're done opened. How we gonna take 'em back?"

Pervis cuts in: "Well, take back what's left. Maybe old Cosper won't notice just a pack gone. If you don't, me and the Cave Man are gonna go to jail, for sure."

"Okay, Okay!" There seems to be agreement all around. Vera gathers the cookies and cigarettes. "Where's the ham?"

"Over here." It's Jake Kennedy. They look around to Jake. He's the biggest of the boys and, Kid figures, the dumbest. He's cut a slice of ham and is feeding his big face greedily. "Hey, that's sure good."

There's a big cheer for Jake as everybody gathers around demanding a slice. They begin grabbing cigarettes out of the carton, then they tear open the cookies and whoop it up. Kid smokes a cigarette. It makes him sick. He eats a slice of ham, and that tastes awful.

Next day, everybody at school knows what happened even before the sheriff drives up and parks out front. He strolls into the principal's office, a pair of handcuffs jangling from his gunbelt. As if that's not scary enough, Kid is the first one called to the office.

A hush falls over the entire school as Kid walks down the corridor alone. It is so quiet his footsteps echo like strokes of an axe. At the office door the principal motions him inside and turns to the sheriff. "This is our resident cave man."

* * * * *

There is no trial, of course. Everybody is clearly guilty. As the townsfolk see it, though, some are maybe less guilty than others. Those girls that broke into the Cosper place are just irresponsible brats. They ought to get their hands slapped, but good. Trouble is, they're both from fine families, as are most of the culprits. The cause of it all, the ringleader, is this Kid from Luna. It takes a real mischief-maker to turn the heads of so many nice youngsters. Too bad old Judge Gibson couldn't just order a good whipping for the damned Kid and a couple others, then turn them all loose.

The office girl at the high school, who seems to like the Kid and can't keep her mouth shut anyway, confides that the principal has talked on the phone about him to someone at the courthouse. And she has sent a copy of grades for "one or two of the kids in trouble" to Judge

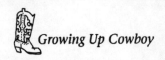

Gibson's secretary in St. Johns. Kid figures his was among those report cards, or she wouldn't have told him. None of this worries him, though. He figures he's free and clear because it's not against the law to have bad grades, and everybody knows he didn't break in or steal anything.

On sentencing day, the Judge is a menacing figure as he glowers down at the trembling offenders. Yet, the folds of his robe cannot hide that he is small in stature, even frail, and his voice is not nearly as threatening as his eyes. It comes out in the breezy tones of a rural cowboy.

"I wish first to address all you parents," he says politely. "It is unfortunate that, due to the irresponsibility of your children, your presence here is necessary. None of this is your fault. When you send kids off to school, you have every right to believe that they will not leave there. Let alone break into an unguarded ranch house. Now, just look at the inconvenience, expense, and embarrassment caused to you. I trust that you will remember it and supervise your boy or girl accordingly."

Kid is squirming. This Judge really knows how to put the heat on.

"As to those of you who are party to robbing the home of Mr. Cosper," his voice is harder now, "this is not a petty offense. It is serious business. Breaking and entering is also involved. I could send each and every one of you to the penitentiary. I could send you to reform school. Or I could sentence you to prison and grant you probation. This would give you an unsavory record for life."

Kid is getting nervous. He can sense tension and apprehension all around.

The Judge continues, "Before I decide what to do, I want this kid they call Cave Man up here."

All eyes turn to the Kid. Mother pats his arm and whispers, "You deserve this. Now tell him the truth, and you'll be all right."

Kid stands before the Judge, knees unsteady. "I believe it was you who led this little expedition to the caves," says Judge Gibson.

Kid's voice cracks with nervousness as he describes events leading to the break-in. He adds, ungallantly, that he and others asked the girls to put back what they had stolen.

That makes no difference, says the Judge sharply. "You're all guilty. How do you think I should punish you?"

Kid swallows, shakes his head, and shuffles his feet. "I dunno, sir."

"You don't know, eh? Well, I'm told you do know quite a bit about these Indians whose caves you prowl around in."

"I've studied their ruins and read a bunch of books on 'em."

"Did they have laws?"

"In a way. They sure had to do what the chief of the tribe or the medicine man said."

"Did any Indians ever disobey that law?"

Kid nods. "Some would beat up others, steal from them. That sort of thing."

"Did the Indians punish those bad guys?"

"You bet."

"What did they do to them?"

"Well, I read that for little crimes they got hung by a toe until it broke or, you might say, pulled away."

There's a stir in the room. Some of the mothers gasp.

"Was it a little crime that you and these other kids perpetrated on Mr. Cosper?"

Kid is trapped. But he knows better than to belittle the break-in. "No sir."

"Bigger, then?"

"Yes."

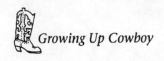

"How did those Indians punish a bigger crime?"

"Besides the toe thing, they might cut off both ears. If it was a woman, they sometimes whacked off her nose."

"Why all this mutilation?"

"Well, for punishment. And so you'd be marked for life as a criminal."

There's a bigger stir in the room. Everybody's getting nervous.

"You've been known to break in and prowl around the homes of these Indians. What kind of crime is that?"

"They're dead, sir." Kid wishes the Judge would call up someone else for a change.

"Their spirit, their very essence, is alive. Otherwise you wouldn't be interested in them. Isn't that so?"

"I never looked at it that way."

"You swiped two priceless old Indian bowls out of a cave by Nutrioso. Is that a crime?"

"Well sure, if those Indians were alive, it would be."

"Do you think it's okay to steal from someone who died yesterday? Last year? Ten years ago?"

"No. That wouldn't be okay. Not that soon."

"How soon would be okay?"

"I guess never," mumbles the Kid.

"For all you know, the spirits miss those bowls. And how many of us would like to have seen the bowls right where their owners left them? Maybe you stole from us, too."

Kid swallows several times. The glory of the pots is fading as he stands before this stinging Judge. And the question he dreads most is yet to be asked.

"Do you understand me?"

"Yes, sir, I do."

"What happened to the pots?"

"I gave one away." Kid closes his eyes and bites his lip.

"And the other?"

Kid is coming close to tears and struggles with the answer. "It fell off a shelf."

"Did it break?"

"In about ten pieces."

The Judge's eyes bore into the Kid, then beyond to sweep the suddenly quiet room, then back to the Kid. "You can sit now."

Kid stumbles back to his seat. He is sweating hard and staring at the floor when he realizes the Judge is speaking again, and his voice has become soft and friendly, almost kindly. "I order you to make restitution to Mr. Cosper. And I order you to go to school. Any absence for the remainder of this year is to be reported to this court. I order you," and his eyes seem again to seek out the Kid, "instead of just reading what you like, to read the books the teachers assign. Maybe you'll improve your grades. And, last, I order you to stay away from those Indian caves, or I'll have your ears and noses, and toes, too." He smiles rather broadly at that, and so does Hank Cosper. Even the principal, who has sat frowning through it all, seems to relax his face.

Outside the courtroom, Jimmy comes up to the Kid and puts a comforting arm around him, like in the old days. "Gosh, damn, for a minute there I thought he was gonna throw the book at you."

"I thought that's just exactly what he did do," mutters the Kid wearily.

(Note: From the standpoint of archeological preservation, one might say our inquisitive Luna Kid was born twenty years too soon. Because of this lamentable cave man episode and hundreds of others of a similar nature, Congress has passed laws making it illegal to remove even surface artifacts from archeological sites in national forests and other federal lands.)

11

Peddling:
Life in the Fast Lane

Peddling, an ancient and once-stable craft, has suddenly gone downhill. Its last practitioners are nowadays about as rare as black-footed ferrets, which, in natural habit, they somehow resemble. Why has peddling declined so? There's no explicable reason. People need peddling now about as much as they ever did. What happened? Perhaps we shall see.

From all appearances, peddling ought to be among the most attractive and satisfying of human occupations. Getting started requires only a small truck. A cheap, used one is quite enough. A little revolving credit at the bank is useful for the first few months but no prerequisite, at least not for those who have the necessary verbal skills for other aspects of the trade. There are many attractive fringe benefits for peddlers: They enjoy that much-prized state of being one's own boss. They travel. They meet interesting people. They do something different each day. They have no responsibility to anybody. They develop impressive

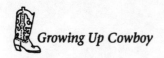
skills in acting, speaking, debate, and negotiation. Being unencumbered by W-2 forms, bank accounts, or real property, they pay no taxes. As they rise to the pinnacle of their profession, they enjoy free lodging and meals.

Given all this, why wouldn't everybody want to be a peddler? Perhaps they would, even now. And perhaps they did back in the heyday of peddling. But peddling, like dancing and singing at the same time, requires abilities and aptitudes possessed by only an elite few. And in modern times those so skilled have likely gone on to bigger and better things.

Luna Valley had its peddler, well known there and in every town from Douglas to Durango. His name was Cass Virden, and he was, by physique, instinct, and aptitude, as well suited to extracting money from people as is any hummingbird for the collection of nectar.

In the first place, Cass was singularly and properly unattractive, his body being constructed in that dichotomous pattern seen most often on jolly men. The shoulders are rounded and somewhat slight. The hips are likewise on the narrow side, whereas all the architecture in between is undulatingly massive in scale. In the case of Cass, even the breasts cascaded, harmonizing with the drooping rolls at the kidney and a slumping belly. (According to one old-timer, Cass had most likely not seen his pecker for ten years.)

Like most everybody out there, Cass generally wore jeans made by Levi Straus. He never buttoned the top two buttons and kept the waistband tucked up under his stomach. The trousers were held in place only by the truss he wore to press back against a hernia, either real, imagined, or affected. (Everyone, himself included, said that Cass was ruptured. Thus, he could count on someone else handling the heaviest sacks and boxes of his trade.)

Above the shoulders, Cass possessed few attractions

with which to offset the ungainliness below. His jowls, though well exercised, sagged like his belly. His nose was wide and rather flat with cavernous nostrils. It spread, blackheaded, across his face. His eyes were small and pale blue, and though the eyeballs themselves appeared bright and darting, their lids were ever lashless and generally tipped with red. He was quite bald. A greying fringe linked oversized ears that, by contrast, bristled widely with a growth of black hair. As if he were not yet noticeable enough, in the heart of cowboy country and in contrast with fashion, Cass always wore a cocky derby and scuffed brown oxford shoes. Oh, yes, he had a false upper plate.

In temperament, Cass was good humored, breezy, quick to laugh with his loud, high-pitched falsetto, or in exuberance, he would often yell like a drunken cowboy. Most folks liked Cass, though a few hated him profoundly. He enjoyed an occasional beer, loved dirty jokes, and loved to gamble so long as there was money in the game. If you had no money, he'd give you money, but there had to be money in the game.

Cass especially liked women, even though as one might expect, he enjoyed little success with them. As long as they were good looking, he liked them young or old, married or single, big or little. He knew (in no biblical sense) every gal along his 200-mile territory. He fell in love with several of them and made no secret of it, celebrating his attachment and the attachee's charms everywhere he went. Smitten, for instance, by the blond daughter of a crossroads filling-station owner, Cass trumpeted her loveliness with such persistence and effect that the business boomed, only to fall off to nothing after a rich Texan came to buy a tank from the fabled mountain beauty and whisked her off to San Antonio. Cass grumbled for months that the Texas millionaire wasn't nearly good enough for his sweetie. But then a cuddly looking sawmiller's wife

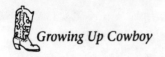

went to work in an eatery down the road, and Cass forgot the blond.

The love of Cass's life, though, was an elegant widow who lived in Luna Valley. By the mid 1940s, according to his own admission, Cass had proposed to her no fewer than thirty-two and a half times. The fractional effort resulted from the day he employed an unwise choice of words and had his face slapped before he could finish his supplication. Cass took pride in that, too, as he went around strutting and bragging about her beauty, goodness, and virtue, adding as partial proof that she had little use for drifters and peddlers.

For audacity, tenacity, and sometimes plain mendacity, Cass beat all. He plied a route between the Gila and San Juan rivers, peddling whatever was in season: melons, pecans, beans, apples, oranges, potatoes, strawberries, piñons, hay, and grain, sometimes even fish, rabbits, and pigeons. All those things he would haul into the high country, selling along the way at an escalating price that varied from house to house. In reports to neighbors, all his clients would inflate the prices they paid Cass in the belief that they mustn't expose him for selling to them cheaper than to anyone else. And most folks along his route took it personal if Cass passed through the vicinity and failed to make a sales call.

It was understood that Cass would spend several days in the valley each trip, taking lodging and meals at the homes of various townspeople. Where he showed up at noon was where he hoped to be invited for a bite of dinner, then back for supper and bed. He never paid, of course, but always left a sack of this or a box of that with his host, and never failed to butter up the hostess with sugary flattery of her beauty, her cooking, her home, or her family.

The Kid's mother mostly considered Cass an insufferable put-on as well as literally and figuratively a dirty fellow, but she tolerated him and liked him for his cheerfulness. Anyway, Cass peddled information, entertainment, and conversation for free. It was Cass who first brought news that a B-25 bomber that buzzed the valley one snowy day, to the excitement of all, had crashed a few minutes later on Mount Ord in Arizona. And folks learned from Cass that the ammo dump supposed to have blown near Alamogordo, knocking most of them out of bed, was really the new kind of bomb that Truman had dropped on Japan. (They earlier learned about the bombing, that also from Cass.) Cass bubbled with gossip, stories, and jokes. And though most adult townsfolk claimed to find him distasteful (it was important not to respect Cass), it seemed fashionable enough to speak of him with some affection just so you tempered that with condescension.

The rural cowboys showed no such reserve in their appreciation of Cass. He loaned them money, tolerated their backtalk, laughed at them and with them, told them about girls, taught them jokes and cards, and (this is crucial) let them drive his truck.

Thus it was that the Luna Kid, who along with motley other rural cowboys had come to view the driving of a truck as the second highest manifestation of manliness (after roping calves, something Kid couldn't do anyway), took off to go peddling with Cass.

* * * * *

The transmission of Cass's Studebaker puts out a hard heroic whine as the Kid surges away from the ramp in compound gear. He double-clutches up to low, and the whine softens. They leave the screaming sawmill behind, but its damp sawdusty smells still fill the truck cab.

The Kid picks up speed slowly before shifting into second. In the seat beside Kid, Cass clicks his tongue,

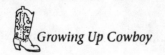

"Don't lug her that way when you got a load. Now put 'er back in low." Kid double-clutches, revving the engine, and shifts down again. It's smooth. Lots better than Cass could have done. Three thousand board-feet of lumber makes a difference.

They climb Frisco Mountain slowly, but the truck has plenty of power in low. On top, the Kid moves to shift up. Cass brushes his hand from the lever. "Keep 'er in low. Save the brakes."

There are no switchbacks going down. But Frisco Mountain has two hairpin curves that the school bus has to stop and back up on. Kid takes them both without stopping, though he figures the outside dual is dangling into the canyon each time. Cass has commenced singing "To Each His Own." He's stopped paying attention to the Kid's driving. Finally they are beyond the corduroys of lovers' lane, and Kid shifts to second, then high, double-clutching meticulously. They're on their way. They go over the hump of Saliz Pass, Kid thrilling to the curves, the whine of the truck crushing and slinging gravel as it powers along.

Nearing Glenwood, Kid looks in question at Cass, who is singing, "You're Breaking My Heart." For some reason, Cass never sings the hillbilly stuff the rural cowboys like. "Wanta stop for coffee?" he asks. "Go on to Frisco," Cass motions straight ahead. "I got a honey there." He sits moody for a mile or so, then breaks into "You'll Never Know Just How Much I Love You." Cass is a pretty good singer, but he goes through only the first verse and chorus of what he's singing, that over and over. Then he stops abruptly and slaps Kid on the knee. "Wow ... Wee ... Woo," he yells. "Wait'll you see this honey." His voice smooths out and breaks into the tune of "You'll Never Know": "I'm gittin' it up ... jist thinkin' a ... bout 'er."

They stop at a little white shack with a peeling sign on

top that spells "Confectionary." Inside, though tiny, it's clean, with oilcloth covering the four tables. Kid can smell coffee, and there's an ice dream dipper on the counter.

They sit. Nobody's there but Kid and Cass. Cass is just saying he'll have to go get her, when the back door opens and a redheaded lady, wearing slacks and a man's faded dress shirt, comes in. She seems flustered. "Oh my," she says. "Gee . . . I didn't see ya pull up."

She reaches under the counter, still looking at them. Her face is curiously flushed to a kind of high pink. If it were cake or ice cream, you'd say it looked good enough to eat. Kid wonders if it's always that way. She pulls out a white apron, loops it over her head, and ties it tightly in back. The apron brings out her large breasts, which curve daintily down toward a tidy waist. A strong woman she is, the Kid can see, and she cares for the little cafe like her own body. With pride.

She looks at Cass. Kid thinks it's a stern look. "You want coffee?"

"Yeah," Cass nods. "Gimme a cup and one for the Kid." Kid is startled that Cass seems awkward with this woman.

She delivers the coffee with steady elegant hands. They are just as pink as her face. Her bare arms are likewise pink. Kid thinks if you take just this one mysterious arm, with its fine rippling curves, and make the rest of a person to match, you'd have one heck of a pretty woman.

She pauses at the table, as though she might say something to Cass, and then moves back behind the counter. Cass glumly sips his coffee.

The woman is staring coldly at Cass. Finally she speaks up, as Kid has known from the start that she was bound to do.

"I'm surprised you've come back here, Cass." She says it without any real tone in her voice.

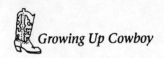

Cass laughs like she's just said something funny. He looks direct at the Kid and winks. "Now what'd I tell you. Didn't I say she's jist as perty as the sun risin'?"

"Yes, ma'am," says the Kid uncomfortably, not liking it that Cass is dragging him into this. "He said somethin' like that."

Kid looks into the Pink Lady's eyes. They are pinched and angry. He tries to signal Cass to ease off. Instead Cass rambles on, "And didn't I say she's got a shape that'd charge up a dead battery?"

The Pink Lady's eyes flare then. In long quick steps she comes around the counter to loom over Cass. Her hands are knotted into fists on arms held straight downward as stiff as wood. "Shame on you, Cass, for talkin' like that. I hate you saying those things. And I hear you're tellin' around on the Gila again that I'm your sweetie and such."

She moves sullenly back behind the counter, pulls off her apron and shoves it back to its drawer, knocking a water glass off onto the plank flooring. The glass bounces, ringing, but doesn't break.

She glares at Cass. Her eyes are icy blue. "You may think you're sweet on me, but I'll say right out I don't even like you. And, Cass Virden, you'd better stop tellin' stories about me or . . . or. . . . " She bites her lower lip and turns her back to them. "Or . . . I'll . . . I'll tell the sheriff. That's just exactly what I'll do, Cass, if you keep it up."

For a moment it's quiet in the cafe. Then she tilts her head slightly toward the Kid. Her voice comes out a little ragged now. Kid can't see the tears, but he can hear them in her soft voice as she speaks more or less toward him. "Ain't it against the law to talk about people behind their backs? To tell lies and all on them?"

Kid finds himself siding with this pretty Pink Lady. "Well, I think it is," he says. "Anyhow it sure had ought to be." He directs a fierce, shaming glare toward Cass, who is alternately tapping the heel and toe of his left foot on the plank floor, making a sound like the creaking of a teetertotter.

At length, Cass stops the tapping and begins to make a statement, "Well, now look here, honey. . . . "

She stamps again. Her back is still toward them. "Darn you to hell, Cass. Now don't say I am when I ain't your honey. If you wasn't so dumb-stupid, you'd know I get mad at you saying that. I ain't even your friend anymore." Her shoulders are quivering, and she commences to sniff.

Kid is still glaring at Cass. "My gosh, Cass," he scolds in a stern loud voice.

Cass stands abruptly. "We'll git goin'," he says. "How much is owed?"

"It's on the house," says the woman, almost whispering, her back still toward them.

They pile back in the Studebaker and head west for Mule Creek. Cass is quiet until they cross the cattle guard at the Arizona line. Suddenly, he pounds the Kid on the knee and yells, "Yow . . . Woo . . . Wee. . . . Ain't she one helluva female?" The Kid nods and grins. He can't help it.

Cass takes the wheel before they start off Blackjack Canyon. The road is little more than a rough ledge blasted off the sheer face of the scariest cliff Kid has ever seen. It's narrow. And both the road and the rock wall above seem to tilt left, toward the canyon side. Cass motions in that direction. "There's a batch of old burnt-out cars way down there. Some say the bodies are still inside. Can't see from here, of course."

Then the truck tire at right front comes up against a high place on the road floor. Cass accelerates over, and the truck tilts, exposing for an instant the deep yawning throat of the canyon all the way to its base, littered with boulders as big as houses. Kid remembers the time when the school bus came up on tourists parked in the middle of the road over Frisco Mountain. They were all crying, scared either to go ahead or turn around. But Frisco Mountain compared to Blackjack Canyon is like a rabbit to a wildcat.

Riding there in Cass's truck, Kid feels dangerously out of place. None of the three, two men and a contraption, belongs here on this awful frowning canyonside. The truck jounces on, clinging to its ledge, Cass still singing cheerfully a bittersweet love song, but the song is coming in fits and starts now.

Suddenly he takes his eyes off the road and looks at the Kid. "Well, whatja think of that little honey back there?"

"She's nice," the Kid feels panic rising from his gut. Only the rocky ruts are guiding the Studebaker along this suicide ledge. "For heaven's sake, Cass, watch what you're doin' here."

Cass glances ahead for an instant, then looks back at the Kid. "You reckon she likes me a little?"

Kid draws upright in the seat and grips the door handle. With a good start he can throw himself out just before they tilt. "Sure, sure, a lot," he blurts quickly, not wanting to prolong the conversation. He begins to hum "Paper Doll," hoping Cass will get back to singing and watching the road. But Cass doesn't pick up the tune; instead, his eyes are on the Kid.

"Yeah, that's what I think, too," he says. "Last time I was in there, nobody else was around. So I said, 'Look here, honey, your old man run out on you years ago. You've been alone too long. You've been workin' too hard here, and there ain't no need. I kin take care of you; so you'd might as well just come away with me!' "

The Studebaker wallows over a rock on the right,

lurching toward the chasm. Kid comes close to a scream. His feet are about to go through the floorboard.

Cass looks ahead just long enough to correct course. Then his eyes swing back to the Kid. "You wanta know what she said?"

"No, Cass, I don't." Kid's teeth are close to chattering. "Hey, watch the road."

"Well, let me tell you what she said! Sure did surprise me, because I thot she'd turn me down right off. She smiled and said, 'They tell me you've got a sweetheart up there in Luna Valley. What you after here anyhow?' "

Cass lets out a long gurgling laugh. To the terror of the Kid, he takes both hands off the steering wheel and pounds his knee with one and the windowsill with the other. "Yeee ... HaHa ... Yoweeewoo. ... What you think of that?"

Kid has the door cracked now. He's ready to jump. "That's too bad," he mumbles through barely open lips.

"Whatcha mean, that's too bad? It's good. She's jealous, dontcha see?"

"Okay, Cass. Just watch what you're doin' now."

"Seein' that she was jealous, I bored right in 'til she finally got mad and booted me out. Ha ... Yee ... Yow ... Woo. ..." His hands are off the steering wheel again. Kid has the door on his side cracked a little more.

The Studebaker picks up speed and lurches. Cass has to grab at the wheel and pump the brakes. "If she's jealous, that means she likes me. Ain't that so?"

"Sure ... sure." Kid, looking straight ahead, is being bounced around on the seat. He has eased a foot into the crack of the door, but now they're going too fast to dare jump out. His mind is on the difference between rolling down the canyon inside the truck or having his soft body flung against sharp rocks of the road and cliff.

Cass presses him. "Don't you reckon she more than likes me? She's sweet on me?"

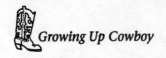

"I reckon," says the Kid.

"Good. We'll stop there on the way back. And you can have a talk with her," says Cass.

Kid scarcely hears him. They're coming up on switchbacks near the end of the canyon. To the Kid, it's not much different from running barefoot down a trail littered with rattlesnakes. "What you talkin' about?" asks the Kid, wetting his lips and easing his door closed again. It could fly open on the turns.

"You're goin' to stop in that lady's place on the way back and have a talk about me and her."

"Shit, Cass. I ain't either."

"Oh the hell you ain't," promises Cass.

"Well, I ain't."

"Okay, okay, look here," says Cass. "I'll bet you ten to one that you can't git her over bein' mad with me."

Now Cass is talking Kid's language. "Ten bucks against one?" asks Kid.

Cass nods. Kid can't imagine what he'll tell the Pink Lady, but ten bucks is ten bucks. Anyway, day after tomorrow is a long way off. And between him and that woman is another crossing of Blackjack Canyon. "I'll take the bet for ten bucks if you'll let me drive back over this canyon instead of you."

"You'll likely kill us both, but I'll chance it," says Cass.

They meet a pickup, luckily just at the runout between switchbacks. Both trucks have to stop and ease by one another. Cass knows the driver. They exchange howdys. "You goin' by Frisco?" asks Cass.

"Yeah. If I live through that damn canyon ahead."

"Expect you'll stop at Millie's for a cup."

"Generally do."

"Tell 'er you saw us at the west end of Blackjack. That'll ease 'er mind. She worries about me, you know.

And keep yore damn hands off her. She's my sweetie. Heh
. . . heh. What that gal's got belongs to me. You ain't gonna
git nothin' there but coffee."

The driver grins. They rev engines. "Tell her old Cass
sends his love."

Coming out of the next switchback, Kid jumps on
Cass. "You hadn't ought to say such stuff. That'll get right
back to her and make her mad all over again."

Cass's laugh is mocking, high-pitched. "Hee . . . hee,
yeah, and put her in just the right mood for when you walk
in day after tomorrow."

That evening, on the Gila, Cass works a deal to trade
2,000 feet of lumber for three tons of watermelon and a
half-ton of cantaloupe. He sells the other thousand feet for
thirty dollars profit.

Kid, who loves to eat watermelons, enjoys the search
for ripe ones in the dusty fields. After a few hours of desert
sun, it gets to be more like work, but there's a kind of hunt
in this, like looking for huge hidden Easter eggs. It might
be fun, except for the nasty tarantulas that have a way of
clinging to or hiding under melons. Loading the truck, Kid
sees a big tarantula on his arm and drops a melon that
glances off the side of Cass's head.

Cass cusses good, and cusses again when Kid swats
the woolly devil off onto his neck. Then Cass flicks the
thing to the ground, and really cusses to high heaven
when the Kid smashes it under a fat watermelon thrown
from the truck, showering Cass with sweet, sticky juice.

* * * * *

By ten in the morning, a worried Kid is climbing the
Studebaker slowly back up Blackjack Canyon. And long
before he tops out, he knows he's more scared of the Pink
Lady than the canyon. At the Mule Creek crossing, though,

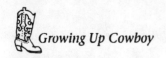

his mind eases a bit because he's getting a plan. Cass is napping on the seat beside him, snoring steadily.

At the junction with the main highway, Kid pulls off the road and wakes Cass to tell his plan. Cass thinks it's a pretty good one and agrees to stay out of sight. Kid suggests maybe dropping Cass off along the road somewhere, then coming back for him, but Cass says he'll just hide out under the tarp 'cause it won't take long anyhow. He stretches out on the cantaloupes, and Kid covers him over. Cass will be comfortable enough. Kid has seen him lie on harder beds than this. And he's well hidden. The lumpy tarp above Cass doesn't look much different from the part that covers the watermelons.

Kid drives on and a while later pulls up at the confectionary. As he gets out of the truck, he hears a buzzing from under the tarp. Cass is sure not suffering any. He's back to sleep already. The Pink Lady looks up as he enters and seems to recognize him but doesn't say anything.

Kid orders coffee. "You remember me? I was here with Cass."

She nods. "Sure do. Hi." She smiles.

Kid is relieved. But after all, she can hardly blame him for what Cass said.

"Cass won't come in, huh? Well he's smart."

"I left Cass on the Gila," says Kid.

She glances out the window, sees the truck and grimaces. "How come?"

"He got beat up."

"Cass. My God. What happened?"

"He'll kill me if I ever tell, and you'd probably kill me, too, because it ain't the sort of things you appreciate."

She sinks into a chair next to the Kid, puts a hand to her forehead, and sighs in the manner of someone expecting bad news. "Okay, what happened?"

"Well, we was at the rodeo yesterday, and he ran into a big guy from Lordsburg. They both seemed to know you and started talkin' about you."

"Oh that damned Cass," breathes the woman. "Who was the guy?"

"I never got his name. But he said something nasty about you. Oh, it wasn't real bad, but it was sure a lie, and it made Cass mad."

"What'd Cass do?"

"He jumped all over that guy. Said nobody could say such a thing around him. I kind of calmed him down, and we was about to leave when the guy described you again, saying 'bitch.'"

The Pink Lady catches her breath sharply. The Kid goes on. "Well, Cass tore into the guy, but you know, Cass ain't a fighter. The guy hit him twice. Cass took the first hit okay, but the second knocked him out cold."

The Pink Lady gives the Kid a shocked stare, then suddenly bursts into tears, nodding her head and sobbing, "Oh poor Cass. And I've been so mean to him."

The Kid gulps down his coffee. "See, I shouldna said anything. Now I've made you feel bad, and Cass is gonna kill me."

She stops crying. "Is Cass okay?"

"He's just a little bloody and raw in the face. He got a crick in his back falling, though, and couldn't make the trip. I'm takin' the melons to Luna. Somebody else'll peddle 'em."

"Well you listen here! You tell Cass that I'm gonna murder him if he don't stop by here right away. I wanta see that darned ole boy to make sure he's okay and give him a great big hug."

"I'll make sure he does, ma'am," says the Luna Kid, and he goes to leave.

The Pink Lady touches his arm. "Those melons you're

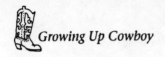

haulin', can I buy just one? It's not the insides I need, but the rind. I never made any preserves this year. This may be the last chance."

"I'll go get one. It won't cost you a penny," says Kid, thinking if she doesn't pay, she won't have to see the melon first. But the Pink Lady follows him out. From a distance, Kid is relieved not to hear Cass snoring. Maybe he's woke up. But as Kid approaches the Studebaker, he hears the buzzing again, like a sawmill two miles off. It could be a fly; anyway, there's not a thing he can do, for the Pink Lady is marching right out with him.

Kid lifts the tailgate and climbs up. To his horror, he senses the Pink Lady pulling herself up behind. She is standing there, crowded against the Kid at the back of the platform. Kid reaches under the tarp and pulls out the biggest melon his hands touch. The buzzing is louder here.

"This okay?" he asks.

"That'll be fine," she says. And just then the buzzing stops, and they hear a third voice. It is a quick "huh," and plainly the voice of Cass.

The Pink Lady glances at Kid sharply. Then her eyes look out across the tarp and settle over in the low place where Cass is laid out. "My God," she says, "look at that."

Kid's first thought is to jump down and run away from this. But he looks, then stares, for there where she's pointing is a tarantula the size of a baseball. It's just climbed out from under the tarp and is crawling to where the tarp slants down toward Cass, right where it naturally picks up the full heat of the sun. There's no question about the location of Cass. The heated tarp has settled round him, petty well outlining the lumps of his head, belly, and feet.

"Just a sec," says the Pink Lady. She climbs down and makes for her little store.

The Kid quickly lifts the tarp. Cass is lying there blinking like a baby just awake. "Don't make a sound," Kid whispers. "She's gonna pick out a melon." As he closes the tarp again, Cass's lips are coming down silently on a bad swear word.

The Pink Lady comes back in no time, walking briskly and carrying a broom. She hoists herself up on the load still holding the broom. Standing on the melons she reaches with the broom and kind of sweeps at the tarantula. It rolls downward and stops in a wrinkle of the tarp just between Cass's jaw and his chest. Then the Pink Lady winds up and brings the broom down in a hard swat. It misses the tarantula, landing instead in the area of Cass's crotch. Dust flies and Kid thinks he hears a hoarse gasp. He wonders how a hit right there might affect a rupture. The next blow lands right over the spider, which draws itself into a ball. "You dirty, filthy thing," cries the Pink Lady, and she whacks away at the tarp as fast as she can swing the broom. By the time she's through, there's nothing left of the tarantula but two wet spots on the tarp. It seems to the Kid that the lumps of Cass's body have flattened out, too.

The Pink Lady's face and arms have flushed out to a kind of blotchy red as she tosses the broom and begins to climb down. "Dirty, filthy thing." She mutters it this time. Then she picks up the broom and storms back inside the confectionary, slamming the door.

The Kid lays a melon on the ground for her, and whispers out of the side of his mouth in the direction of Cass. "Sit tight. I'm gittin' us out of here quick before she comes back."

Cass is still gasping when Kid stops the truck and pulls him from under the tarp. His nose is bleeding. Kid finds his upper plate between two cantaloupes about three feet from his head. Cass gradually gets enough breath to commence to cuss. He dabs at his nose and cusses and pants all the way to Glenwood.

12

Saga of
Mules and Old Men

Two of the least numerous but most dominant creatures of the Mogollon Breaks are people and horses. Even rarer, but yet well represented, is a kind of infertile subspecies of each. On the one hand, we have the crusty old mountain bachelor. Energized by his own prejudice, jealousy, possessiveness, and intolerance, he is everlastingly self-righteous, contrary, single minded, abusive, gossipy, and cranky. On the other hand, we find his kindred spirit or alter ego, the mountain mule. Tough, crafty, introverted, smug, resentful, brooding, he or she is doubtless the most undependable, ungrateful, and unpredictable domestic animal of the earth.

Seems almost unfair that both man and mule have to carry around so much antisocial baggage. Why are they this way? Is it the isolation and loneliness of life in the mountains? The legacy of rarefied air? Too much hard work in the sun? Is it a cause or an effect that both these imperfect eccentrics are at the end of their lineage? Who

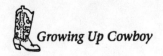

knows. Perhaps some answer can be found in the narrative that follows, in which old man and mule interact to provide the Luna Kid with a wrenching trauma and the highest adventure of his young life.

* * * * *

According to Joe, the earth is almost flat. It's like a sawmill slab that has bark on one side and is sawed smooth on the other. The bark side is the mountains, and the flat side is the plains. A guy moves across the earth just like an ant on a board, and like an ant, he doesn't know whether he's upside down or right side up. As long as he doesn't know which is which, there's no difference. But Joe remembers a guy who figgered it out. That fellow never again left his house on certain days of the month unless he tied himself to a rope. He reckoned those were upside-down days, and he was likely to fall clean off the earth. Also on those days, everything that fellow said came out backward. To understand him you had to wait until he got done talking—then try to play the words forward in your mind.

"It 'uz enough to scramble your brain, but good," recollects Joe.

"The other end of that rope, what did he tie that to?" asks the Kid.

"Well, an anvil or somethin', I reckon," says Joe.

"Wouldn't that anvil fall, too?" asks the Kid. "And just drag him, hollering, that much faster?" Joe frowns at the Kid. He doesn't like back talk and confusion.

Joe and the Luna Kid are stopped beside Campbell Blue Creek. They squat in the shade of willows long enough to open a can of Spam and eat it between soft, dry slices of baker's bread. Now they've moved back out of the shade because even in July, it's cold at nine thousand feet unless the sun hits you. Now Joe begins to carry on about gravity being the same thing as suction. The Kid lies back in the grass. Flies buzz, and the sun seeps in through his grey shirt and levis to warm his skin.

Roanie and Joe's bay, Pete, are tied across the creek. Pete is unsaddled and wears only a rope halter because Joe thinks he ought to relax at noon the same as people. Besides, Joe doesn't want to chance his saddle getting scratched. Pete's a pretty pony with a mane and tail lighter than his body hair, but he's way too fat. Everybody knows that if Pete ever strains, he'll founder and die. Maybe even Joe knows it, because he never trots or lathers old Pete. And up a steep trail, Joe pulls to a halt every fifty feet or so. That's no problem for the Kid. Roanie is older and lazier now.

Anyway, Roanie has to pack most of the tools because Joe won't load Pete or risk buffing his new custom saddle. He carries a double-bit axe in a saddle scabbard and a canteen wrapped in burlap. That's all. He doesn't even tie a slicker on behind because that would cover and hide the padded hand-tooled cantle. Kid has to bring along the heavy leather saddlebags, plus his own axe. On days when it's needed, he also has the awkward, hateful job of balancing a crosscut saw on his right shoulder.

Joe drones on. He's staring across the creek where he can see Pete, also the saddle that he has carefully and lovingly placed across a smooth log of just the right size. Joe is feeling warm and good now, his watery blue eyes fixed on his horse and saddle. He's surveying them with interest and pride, the way a regular man might look out over a gathering of his posterity.

"Brag on his horse and saddle, and you'll get along fine with old Joe," the assistant ranger, Owen, had told the Kid. Maybe Kid has laid it on a little too thick, because now it seems Joe has come to expect the praise. The old man would talk nonsense for a while, then fish for compliments. At the moment he has run down on the flat earth

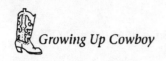

and gravity and suction.

Joe takes out a pocketknife and begins whittling. "I rode past the post office Saturday, and five or six people came runnin' out to see that saddle. It's all over town now. Everybody knows I shelled out three hundred bucks, and they want to see what I got. Nobody around this country ever spent that much on a saddle before. It *is* a perty thing. Ain't it?"

"Mighty nice," says the Kid.

"Them fellers in the saddle shop couldn't believe their eyes." Joe has some chewing tobacco caught under his false teeth. He rolls the upper plate downward with his tongue. There's a sucking clack, then he spits. "When I walked in there and told 'em what I wanted, they jist about shit. They thought I never had ten cents to my name, and then I plunked down three hundred dollars. They about shit. I was tied up at the office the other day, and the ranger's wife, she come across the road to see it. She said it was the pertiest outfit she'd ever seen.

"And, then, it wasn't ten minutes later that stink-mouthed Tommy Earl came by on his bronc-eyed mule." Joe's voice is getting high-pitched and irritated. "You know what that little freak said, right to my face? He said a powder-puff saddle is a good fit for a pony that's too fat even to butcher. If I could a got my hands on that contemptible lizard, I'd have made half-breed fur fly from here to Springer."

Kid is surprised. He's seen Tommy only once, a little dark man sitting low in the saddle, with a hump between his shoulders. Even from a ways off, Kid had noticed deep wrinkles in a sad face. But Tommy never looked any more Indian than Joe, and Joe's red skin would sunburn faster than a white hog.

"I never heard tell that Tommy was a half-breed," says the Kid.

"Well, maybe he ain't in fact," says Joe. "I reckon any respectable half-breed would be a good deal smarter than Tommy and half as ugly."

Joe's eyes are still studying his saddle. "Did ya ever see toolin' as fancy as them cowbells they carved across the skirts of that there saddle?"

"No sir. Not as fancy," answers the Kid.

"And I never seen saddle swells streamlined just the way them are. Did you?"

The sun is hitting the Kid just right. He's warm now. He thinks what a nice spot it is here, with the singing creek, the tall redtop, and smell of willow and spruce. The flies buzz, the birds chatter and chirp. He can hear a breeze brushing and gasping through aspen on the hill behind. The only unpleasant sound is Joe's whiny voice and the clack of his teeth as he chews and sucks.

The Kid has heard enough of this to last a while. He's tired of hearing about that saddle. "Well," Kid says, "it may seem funny, but those swells kind of remind me of a rattlesnake coil, and the horn is its head up there fixing to strike." Joe stops chewing and stares at the Kid in surprise. Then he looks back at the saddle with a frown. Kid can see that Joe doesn't appreciate anybody seeing snakes on his saddle.

Kid learned the first day they worked together that Joe doesn't have a sense of humor. He isn't much of a worker either. If they can ride six or eight miles of fire trail a day, Joe is satisfied. Unless they find a tree or rock-slide across the trail, there's not much work in this, just cutting some brush and branches and checking for washouts.

Daddy used to contract to build fire trail for the Forest Service. That's work, Kid knows. But maintaining trail is pretty much a matter of just riding it. If only Joe were not so tiresome and whiny. A pity, Joe might have been something like T.J. Some of his ideas are as queer as T.J.'s,

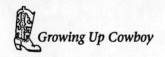

or more so, but nowhere near as interesting. Joe's feelings are tender, like a match ready to strike. Anybody as touchy as Joe is dull and no fun. You couldn't carry on with him like you could with T.J. or old Cass Virden. Come to think of it, Kid doesn't know any old bachelors that you can cut loose and talk back to or argue with. He wonders if living with a woman doesn't take some of the backwardness and put-on out of a man. Maybe the experience greases a guy up so he runs better.

The ranger is sending him out to the Blue Range next to ride trail with Tommy. Kid wonders if Tommy will be any different. At least he won't have a fancy saddle and a lard-ass horse for a pet. Tommy rides a battered old high-back cavalry saddle atop a big, bearded mule that's as lean, mean, and muscular as any the Kid has ever seen.

* * * * *

Tommy isn't around when Owen drops off the Kid with bedroll and Roanie at the tent in Hannigan Meadows. Kid has heard that Tommy is even harder to get along with than Joe. Owen's advice comes out all don'ts: "Don't ask questions. Don't talk much. Don't worry if he won't talk. He's crazy about mules, so don't say anything bad about Redeye. He hates Joe, so don't say anything good about Joe. If Tommy likes you, he'll treat you fine. You'll learn a lot. If he don't like you, he'll run you off in ten days, and we'll put you back to ridin' with Joe."

Kid has an idea Owen is feeling uneasy about leaving him there. "I want you to stay plumb away from that mule of Tom's. He's wicked, and nothing for you to mess with. Nobody but Tom can touch him. Just you keep your distance."

Late in the evening, Kid is stretched out on his bunk when he hears Tommy ride up and unsaddle his mule. It's getting dark in the tent as Tommy opens the flap and stares in at the Kid. Kid nods and stands. "Howdy," he says.

Tommy glares. "I was expectin' a grown-up," he says to himself. His voice is nasal, nearly squeaky.

He ambles into the tent. He's a short man, slight of build, the hump on his back forcing his head forward until it seems to grow out of his chest rather than his shoulders. His legs seem too short, even for a small man, and his arms too long. He holds the latter bent at the elbow, as though to make them look shorter. His nose hooks down toward an indrawn mouth, squared off by deep vertical lines to each side; Kid can't imagine a smile there. Tommy's eyes are black and small. His felt hat is uneven and scruffy in appearance. It's worn through in spots at the creases and tilted back enough to reveal a pale and wildly wrinkled forehead. Joe was sure right about one thing: Tommy is about as ugly as humans come.

Tommy turns his back to the Kid and speaks up clearer. "There's wood to git and water to carry." Kid knows he is off to a bad start with Tommy.

Kid learns early next day that the little guy may be rude and ugly but he's made of springier stuff than Joe. It's not yet light in the cold tent when Tommy's muttered "them horses need gittin" brings Kid out of his bedroll and sets his warm feet on the cold floor. By seven o'clock they're on their way down Grant Trail. Kid doesn't like it much. He's paid only from eight to five. But what can you do?

Fire trails dropping off the east face of the Blue Range are not quite as spectacular as the famous mule trails into the Grand Canyon, but they're close. In fact, Blue Canyon from rim to river is about as deep as the Grand. Luna Kid soon learns that these wild, plunging, sometimes torturous trails simply cannot be ridden down and back in a legal, genteel, eight-hour day. Gentleman Joe, with his

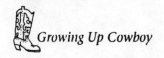

streamlined saddle and pampered pony, might get into the Blue, but Kid begins to doubt he could ever get out.

Each day with Tommy seems more of a challenge and an accomplishment. And the longer the day, the more they see of the wild and beautiful slopes and canyons. Kid's resentment at the long, unpaid hours vanishes as he comes to realize this. But still, Tommy doesn't seem to warm up.

Tommy rides ahead, his hump giving the impression of a deep slouch in the saddle. He never looks to the rear, rarely speaks, and never addresses the Kid directly. When they stop to clear trail, Kid watches and listens to Tommy for signals. Sometimes Tommy will mention out loud to himself that a certain branch could catch a man's hat or a rock could cause a stumble in the dark. Kid takes it as instructions to cut the branch or move the rock.

By about the sixth day of keeping up with Redeye, Roanie is worn out and foot sore. Kid doubts that any horse could keep up with Redeye for long. The mule is rugged and rank. He moves like a machine, muscles rippling along his legs and rump. He never coughs through his scraggly mule beard or lathers, and never breaks out of a walk. Even so, Kid often has to kick Roanie into a trot to keep up.

It's clear to the Kid that Tommy's devotion to his mule is a one-way street. Tommy has to wear thick leather chaps because Redeye scrapes up against anything that scratches. It may be brush, barbed wire, or cactus, and it's always Tommy who gets scratched, never the mule.

Tommy has to dismount and lead Redeye across logs because the cussed mule won't step over like a horse but insists on jumping. When Tommy stays in the saddle, the mule jumps twice as high as needed, then comes down stiff legged, pile-driving Tommy's privates (assuming the old codger has any). If there's a low branch, Redeye sidesteps against the tree it's on, forcing Tommy to duck or get scraped off. Redeye will snort and rear at a rabbit or grouse, or anytime there's the slightest excuse.

But Redeye doesn't always get away with his foolishness. Tommy is no slouch at handling mules. He holds a tight rein, especially getting on and off. He seems to know what the mule is going to do and talks to him like he is coaxing a smile from a baby, and when he does that, some of the fierce craftiness leaves the eyes of the big mule. Kid wonders—this mule is plenty capable of killing Tommy, and there is often a danger in his eyes. Oh, it's not the mindless violence you'd see in a mean horse but a cunning danger. If you were foolish enough to get behind him, Redeye would laugh while kicking your head off. But sometimes the Kid has another thought about Redeye: he torments Tommy to get attention. And more than Tommy's ropes and halters and gates, it's the stroking and petting and soft words that keep him, for this is a critter that would like to be free. Without Tommy there would be no Redeye. One way or another he'd be gone.

But there's more between these two. Some kind of kinship. Maybe Tommy loves Redeye and Redeye puts up with Tommy because they're both freaks and outcasts without hope of posterity. Anyway, if it makes Tommy happy to pet and kissy-poo a stinking mule, more power to him. Tommy is clever and tough, and he's a worker. In a lot of ways he has it over people who look better. Little old humpback though Tommy is, Kid never really feels sorry for him except when he leans over to stroke and baby talk old Redeye.

Webb Dillon, the kindly game warden at Hannigan, knows Tommy pretty well, and he likes mules himself. One day Webb notices that Roanie is getting tired, and he has an offer for the Kid. "I've got a filly mule that needs exercise," he says. "I'd be much obliged if you'd ride her down every now and then. She's sometimes contrary gettin' on, but she's plumb gentle."

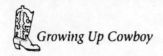

Kid agrees. So, next morning, under the interested eye of Tommy, he saddles Clementine. She's a pretty little pinto mule, so short that leading her up to the first gate, Kid notices two shallow furrows on either side of the trail. Tapaderos below the stirrup are dragging in the dust.

Kid well knows that some saddle mules hate letting the rider on. He can't imagine trouble with this little lady, even though the game warden hinted at it. She'll be no harder to mount than a bike. Kid flings a rein up over the left side of her neck. As he moves toward the stirrup to swing on, she takes one step forward, then another. Kid tugs the rein to stop her, and she swings around facing him. He tries to mount again. The results are the same: she steps forward until he has to tug the rein, then maneuvers her body away, leaving him nothing to mount.

Kid glances toward Tommy. He is watching. Kid studies the problem. The only way to mount this contrary little snot would be to stand in front of her. And how in hell can you reach the stirrup standing in front? Kid is embarrassed. Tommy is not fidgeting yet, but he's staring.

There's only one thing to do: this time Kid doesn't pull the rein as Clementine comes by. Instead, he grabs for the saddle horn. Now he's ahold of the saddle horn, trotting alongside the mule, skipping and hopping, trying to get his left foot into the stirrup. He misses and nearly falls. He swears and pulls Clementine to a stop. Canteens bounce and dust flies.

Kid looks around for Tommy, who he hopes has started out already and won't be looking back. Tommy is sitting there on Redeye, watching. He's tilted his hat back. There's an expression on Tommy's face the Kid's never seen. He's enjoying this. Redeye is watching, too. Kid imagines a jeering expression on his dished face.

The Kid swears. He's mad at Clementine but madder at Tommy who could be offering to help instead of staring like a slobbering spectator at a freak show. "You goddam pea-brained little dwarf son of a bitch." He swears at the mule, but maybe Tommy will get the idea. Why would anybody call a bitch a son of a bitch?

This time the Kid is ready. He's standing on his right foot and has the left one pointed directly at the spot where the stirrup will be as Clementine goes by. He simultaneously grabs the saddle horn and kicks his foot into the stirrup. Suddenly, Clementine is running and the Kid is hanging on to the horn. One foot is in the stirrup and the other springs along in a series of looping hops, trying to swing over the saddle, getting a little closer each hop, and finally swinging aboard. Quickly Kid pulls in the reins and braces himself for the jarring stop, but the little mule has already slowed to a trot. An instant before, she controlled the power and leverage. Now the Kid does. She seems to know this. The Kid is almost disappointed. He'd hoped to jerk a few well-deserved bruises into her feisty little mouth with the bridle bit.

Kid pulls Clementine to a stop and looks around. Tommy is farther away now but still watching. Kid waits for him. Suddenly Tommy reaches a hand up to his weather-beaten hat and doffs it toward the Kid. The creases around his mouth are softer now. There's a hint of a smile on his leathery face.

Once on their way, Kid finds the little mule not bad riding. She's lively, responsive, smooth of gait, long winded, and tough in the climbs. But after they stop to clear some trail, Kid has to go through the same hopping, flying, looping, leg-roll to get mounted. On first try, Kid loses it all when Clementine runs through the trees, but on the second run he manages to heave himself into the saddle. Once again Tommy is a silent, hat-doffing, half-grinning spectator.

By noon, Kid has repeated the acrobatics four times. They are sitting on the edge of a bank looking down on

Fish Creek and eating canned beans and vienna sausage. The creek is clear and fairly slow. It's a warm day and a good place to sit. Trout swim leisurely in the pools below. To the north, across Black River, rises the long high ridge of the White Mountains, creased here and there by forks of the river, otherwise almost featureless. Where the ridge rises or falls, it gets a name. There's Mount Ord and Mount Baldy, two of Arizona's highest peaks, and farther along, Greens Gap and Williams Valley. Down the Blue Range, across the Black, and on to the horizon, every rise and swale is whiskered over with trees. There's scarcely a fence from here to there, and not a rock or clearing shows.

Tommy and the Kid take their time even though the mules haven't been watered. It's nearly straight down to the creek here. They'll have to ride a ways to find a way out. There's no hurry. It's not such a long trail to cover today, and Tommy seems to be enjoying the spot.

The Kid is getting an idea. The longer they sit, the better shape it takes in his mind. Finally he says to Tommy, "I've figured out how to get on that durn mule without running a footrace." Tommy looks a question at him but says nothing.

Kid unties Clementine and leads her up to the edge of the drop-off. "Okay you slippery little sow bitch," he says to her. "Now let's see you run away." He steps around to the side and stabs at the stirrup with his left foot.

Without hesitation, Clementine surges forward, propelling herself and the terrified Kid into outer space. Kid feels himself flipping over, then sliding and bouncing. Suddenly he's upside down, halfway under the mule, and all the way into icy water. The mule flips catlike above him. The Kid rolls out. He tries to stand, but he doesn't have footing. He splashes, staggers, and falls backward at the grassy edge of Fish Creek. He opens his eyes. His glasses are okay. He moves his arms and legs. They don't feel broken.

Kid hears a noise. It is coming from above and sounds something like bellows blowing a fire. He sees the head of Tommy then, peering over the bank. Tommy's mouth is open wide, exposing snaggled teeth and a fleshy cavity dripping saliva. He is laughing in breathless explosive bursts that come into the Kid's ears over the sounds of the creek. Kid looks around for the mule. Clementine is contentedly drinking just upstream. Black mud coats the saddle, and both canteens are missing. He sees one floating further down the creek.

The Kid shakes his head in disbelief. "Oh shit," he says. Tommy cuts loose laughing and wheezing again. Kid has had enough of this. He'll cuss Tommy good. He looks up into the gleeful face. He can't say a word. He looks away quickly. He comes close to grinning. To hide it, he lets loose a raft of swearing in the direction of Clementine. Then he turns toward Tommy and shakes his fist. Tommy, he who never laughs, is carrying on like a fool gone to heaven.

Kid is wringing out socks when Tommy controls himself and calls down. "Ain't that water too cold fur swimmin'?"

It's the first time he has spoken straight-on to the Kid. Kid doesn't know why, but after that bruising day on Clementine, old Tommy becomes talkative as a blue jay. Kid is surprised to learn that he can spin a yarn a whole evening long. And now that he feels like talking to the Kid rather than at him, he is inclined to go on and on, outcussing any sawmiller along the way.

Tommy fashions himself as some kind of a tough who's never taken abuse from anybody. He is fond of quoting himself, and to hear him tell it, he's uttered hundreds of dire threats directly into the faces of bosses, adversaries, and competitors during his lifetime. Listening to him, Kid wonders if Tommy hasn't muttered a few

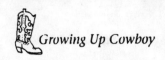

threats against the Kid himself because Tommy can't get even a little irritated without speculating about how so-and-so will look with his head caved in, a knife in his belly or windpipe, or what tone his scream might take during an operation on his scrotum.

One day Kid and Tommy are riding side-by-side across Double Cienega, and Tommy is ranting on about Joe and Pete. "A fat-ass ridin' a teddy bear in a dingle-dude saddle," as Tommy puts it. "You could take an' kill old Joe in his own easy chair with his arms folded, and 'twouldn't even be murder."

Tommy's gone a little too far. "Wait a minute," says Kid. "If you do that, it's sure murder even if the law don't catch you."

"No it ain't," insists Tommy. "You could kill Joe jist the way they got Kelton Fuzbaugh down there in the Clifton jail. He was a two-bit thief, a public nuisance, and a coward like Joe. So one day they blindfolded 'im and told old Kelton, 'You're gonna die now for yore sins.' Then they took a sharp piece of ice and run it around his throat from ear to ear. You know what he done?"

Kid nods. It's a typical Tommy story. Unbelievable in a way but kind of interesting.

"That sumbitch died."

"You could commit a perfect crime that way," says Kid.

"I aim to. On old Joe. Heh, heh."

"Well I wanta see it," says the Luna Kid, thinking that'll be the day old Joe himself "jist about shits."

One of Tommy's most interesting tales is about how he found Redeye up by Gallup. "A mine closed and sold off their cart horses. It was a sorry-looking bunch. Some horses was nearly blind from workin' in the dark so long. Then I saw this mule, sleek as a summer calf, and he had bright red eyes. An old gent who fed the company horses told me Redeye had a slick trick that kept him out of the mines. The horses would work two days, then rest one day. Accordin' to this feller, Redeye was always with the resting bunch because he'd undo the gate at night with his teeth, go through, then push it shut, and slide the latch back again.

"I've had mules all my life. I've known 'em to open gates, but I never heard tell of one shuttin' it again. Now I always put a chain or wire around any wood gate that Redeye's behind. If I didn't, he'd be gone like a fart in a cyclone.

"Redeye was about six years old then, and broke to ride. That seemed strange in a cart horse. I'm sure now he'd been on a stock train that derailed some years ago north of Zuni. One of the cars was full of horses bound for a glue factory in Texas, mostly old nags, of course. All the horses either got killed or took off and run away."

Tommy points to a faint off-color stripe running from the shoulder down along the leg of Redeye, almost to his knee. Kid hadn't noticed it. "That's a gunshot scar," continues Tommy. "There wasn't much grass the year of the wreck, so the Indian Service come in with airplanes and shot the strays. They pert-near killed old Redeye. He must have come close to bleedin' to death. That bullet went through a mighty big artery below his shoulder there. Redeye is scared loco of airplanes. Learnin' that lesson just about finished me off. Anytime I hear a plane comin', I git off and tie him up, pronto."

"Why would anybody want to send a saddle-broke mule off to the glue factory?" asks Kid.

Tommy looks keenly at his mule. He admires Redeye, but from his answer Kid wonders if he's not also a little envious. "That mule's big and mean," says Tommy. "There's not much he fears. I reckon he killed somebody once or came near to it. Sometimes you can see that in his eyes.

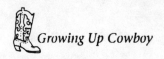

Redeye was on that train because somebody was mighty scared of him."

"Hell, I'm scared of him," says Kid.

"Everbody is 'cept me," says Tommy proudly.

"How come you ain't?"

"Well, he worked in a circus once."

"What's that got to do with it?"

"Heh, heh. I just pull his beard now and then, and he gits gentle as a baby."

Tommy's talking foolishness again.

13

The Mule That
Never Returned

L ate in July, spotty rains bring lightning. One day
  Tommy and Kid see black smoke over the timber
somewhere above PS Knoll. The day is hot and dry. The
smoke gets higher and blacker. Tommy fumes about it.
"We'd better ride over to Reno lookout and have a look,"
he says.

At Reno, the towerman and his horse are gone.
Tommy and Kid climb the tower. The fire is below them,
across Black River. It's a fierce one and spreading fast in
pine and brush country. Tommy rings Owen at Alpine.
Owen is just leaving for the fire and says the Reno ranger
is already on his way down. He tells them to man the tower
until supper, then head off to the fire. "Bring all the gear
you can. Try to be at the Black by dark. That's a tough trail
to follow at night."

There's fresh water on the hillside below the tower.
Kid goes down to fill the canteens and walks right past the
spring. It takes him nearly an hour to find water. They're

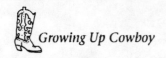

late leaving the tower. Finally, just at dusk, they take the trail into dark woods, Redeye and Roanie well loaded with rations and gear. The fire can't be seen from here, but Kid can smell it in the evening air, sometimes only faintly, but now and then in low pockets the smoke comes up strong enough to burn his eyes.

At first, the trail lies clean and clear ahead like a plowed ditch, but as the light fades, it begins to disappear in places. Kid is riding in front, steering Roanie. They lose the trail. Soon they're in deep brush and logs. Tommy curses. They get off and lead. Now they're about a thousand feet lower than the tower. The forest is not as thick, but the light is gone. It's the darkest part of night in the mountains, midway between twilight and starlight. They are lost.

They lead on, looking for signs of the trail. It's slow going. They stumble and cuss. The timber is thinner here, and there aren't so many logs, but now they're into rocks.

Suddenly Tommy yells at the Kid: "Hold it there. Don't take a step."

"What's the matter?"

"Redeye won't budge. Somethin's wrong. Jist sit down and stay put."

Tommy doesn't often give orders that way. Kid is impressed enough to do just what he says. It's cold on the mountainside. Kid begins to shiver. "How about a fire?" he asks.

"Nothin' doin'. A fire now would ruin our eyes for the whole night. Sit still, and maybe in a while we can see to git off of here."

Slowly, trees begin taking a blotty shape on each side of the Kid. He can see a branch here and there, but the edge of everything still seems to bleed off into dark pockets and shadows. Directly ahead, there's only an eerie wall of darkness. Kid watches the blank wall, wondering. After a while, he thinks he can see a line of trees. Incredibly, they are far away.

Tommy speaks up then. "Shit's afire. We're sittin' on a bluff. We'll have to stay here until light."

Kid shudders. He could have led dumb Roanie right off that cliff. Redeye saved them all. Now they're a mile or more off the trail. Kid asks again about a warming fire.

"I figger that forest fire is somewheres below us, jist across the river," says Tommy. "I don't want nobody down there seein' a fire up here. They'll think we got lost."

"Well, we are lost."

"You're the one lost. You 'n that damned clubheaded Clydesdale. I ain't lost."

Kid shivers on. Tommy sleeps, but now and then he jerks awake. At dawn, Kid wakes Tommy. "Should we get goin'?"

"Not fur two hours. We come in too early, an' they'll know for sure we laid out up here."

Kid shakes his head. Old ugly Tommy doesn't have much to justify all that pride.

Once down on the Black, they find the trail and make good time in the direction of the fire, which is beginning to flare up again as the breeze rises. They ride toward smoke that boils and billows a thousand feet straight up until they find a camp on the river. Owen is there.

"We worried about you," he says.

"We was late gettin' started last night so we waited 'til early this mornin'," says Tommy.

Owen stares at them. They're dirty and haggard and hungry-looking. Kid thinks he's not fooled. "Well," he says, "we better git to work makin' a fire line." There's no mention of his orders of last night. Owen maybe understands more about this pride business than the Kid does.

Owen leaves them building a line around the southwest perimeter. The fire is largely burned out here and has

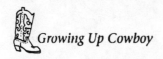

followed the wind to the north. In the afternoon, they link up with another crew and stop to rest. Suddenly the shadows have disappeared, and it's almost dark around them. They can hear a roar far off. "The fire's crowned out and headed across Loco Knoll," says somebody in a hushed voice. The crackling lasts maybe fifteen minutes as ash begins to shower around them.

By evening, the fire seems to be lying low, but rumors are flying along the line. It's out of control to the north, and some guys are cut off and surrounded, they hear. There's still no road in, no bedrolls, no rations, no bulldozers. Somebody says the fire's already burned 16,000 acres. Some are saying it's under control, and others are saying there's hell to pay, then word comes that Owen wants Tommy and Redeye up in the northeast sector. Trees have fallen across the fire line. There being no bulldozer, they want Redeye to snake the logs out with a rope.

The sound of it worries Kid, who's glad they never asked for Roanie. But Tommy's eyes are bright and proud as he mounts Redeye. "I'll see yu at supper," he tells Kid.

About an hour later, Kid hears the faint sound of an engine. His first thought is relief that they've finally brought equipment in. He doesn't like the idea of Tommy having to do a machine's work. It gets louder. It's not a bulldozer but a little Forest Service spotter airplane out of Springer. It comes in low over them.

Now the Kid hears somebody say there'll be no road in before tomorrow. After a while, a crew of tree trimmers comes down the line carrying rations. They've walked in from Beaverhead, and they say a guy up the line is hurt. A stretcher crew is on the way to carry him out. Then a message comes down that Owen wants the Kid.

Kid saddles Roanie without enthusiasm and hits a trot up the fire line. He figures they probably need more help to snake out logs. He rounds the burnt-off knoll and hears the sound of a scuffling animal. Roanie raises his head and stares. Redeye is tied there to a tree. He is struggling against the halter and pawing in cadence. Occasionally he kicks both hind legs rearward. He's either scared as hell or mad as hell.

There's a knot of men, including Owen, just outside the fire line. Owen motions the Kid over. Tommy is lying there on his side. His knees are bent and drawn up toward his chest. His head is between his elbows. There's blood on his arms and face.

Owen whispers hoarsely to the Kid. "Damn mule went haywire and pawed old Tom. He wants to talk to you. He says you'll understand it's not the mule's fault." Owen shrugs. "It don't make sense."

Kid doesn't know how to answer. He kneels beside Tommy, who blinks his recognition. "You okay, old feller?"

"Yeah." Kid thinks Tommy is hurt pretty bad, though there's no sign of pain. His voice is faint and slow but clear enough. "Take Redeye back to camp. Don't let nobody mess with him 'til I git there."

"You bet I will."

Tommy's eyes are closed. As they carry him off, Redeye suddenly lets out a wild bellow; it's halfway between a scream and a nicker.

"I'm gonna kill that son of a bitchin' mule," growls Owen. "There's no place in this business for a mean bastard like that. I should've took him away from Tom long ago."

It's scary hearing Owen talk like that. He's a tough ex-cowboy and rancher. He may do what he says. Kid is not about to tell Owen why Redeye spooked at the airplane. It'd only make him that much more suspicious of the mule. Kid is angry at Redeye. He deserves a good whipping for hurting Tommy, but for the first time, Kid feels a pang of pity.

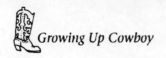

Kid swallows, "Don't worry about the mule. I'll take care of him," he says.

Owen looks at Kid sharply, "You been handlin' that mule?"

Kid nods.

"I told you to stay plumb away from him."

"Well, I thought you meant just his hind end. Hell, sir, I rode the game warden's mule. She's rougher than Redeye any day."

Owen stares at the Kid in some surprise. Kid's never before talked back to him. Then he says, "All right, let's see you handle him."

Kid is sweating. He's in a jam, and there's no reason for it. He hates the damn mule, but somehow the thought of what Owen might do to Redeye has got Kid into this. He'd rather walk through lightning in a flat than touch this mule, but some things you have to make yourself do, like riding that bull calf years ago. Owen is watching. Kid's got to reassure him, or it may be curtains for Redeye, who has settled down some but is still ranting around.

Kid looks the mule in the eyes where he's learned to read Redeye's mood. They seem darker red and have a dull expression, kind of stricken. Maybe Redeye realizes he's hurt Tommy. He'd be the one to know, having, as Tommy said, hurt somebody before. As Kid approaches and puts a hand out, the mule stops fighting the rope and tenses. His eyes flare and the ears lie back. He's not taking to the Kid.

If poor old Tommy were here, he'd be baby-talking Redeye right now. And just look what he got for being nice to this brute—a bloody head. Kid has a different idea. He'll give Redeye a good whipping. He deserves that, and it'll impress Owen. Kid gets his quirt, walks up on Redeye, and grabs for the halter. Redeye backs up against the rope and bares his teeth, ears still back. Kid's hand brushes Redeye's beard, and Tommy's words come back to him, "Pull his beard and he's like a baby."

Kid grabs the beard, and to his astonishment his fingers close around a steel ring in the lower lip. Redeye freezes. Somebody has put a ring through Redeye's lip. Holding him there he's tame as a baby all right. It's a strange sensation to touch this hated mule and find him helpless. Redeye's ears have come forward. He's relaxed and his eyes have rounded. They're not so fierce and cunning anymore. He seems to be saying, "Now you've got me, do as you please."

Still holding the ring, Kid reaches out to Tommy's saddle and pulls it off. He can't ride Redeye and hold his beard, too. He looks around at Owen, who is still watching.

"He's all right," Kid tells Owen. "But we'd better let him stand awhile. Untie him now, and I'll have to whip him good or he'll take after those guys who carried off Tommy. I hate whipping old Tommy's mule when he ain't here." Kid says it in an offhand way.

Owen doesn't object. "Okay, you want that mule, you can have him. Just you keep him away from me, or I'll kill the son of a bitch."

Later in the day, Redeye is calm. Kid feeds him, giving the ring a tug or two. Finally Kid leads a docile Redeye to water. Now he understands how Tommy guessed about the circus.

By noon next day, the fire is secure, and they hear that Tommy's on the mend with "about forty stitches" in his ear and cheek. Poor old Tommy will be even uglier now.

Late that evening, but well before dark, Kid gives Redeye's beard a good tugging, then leads him back to Reno lookout behind Roanie. Joe is manning the lookout now. Kid is to stay there with him as smoke-chaser while Tommy mends.

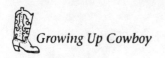

* * * * *

A few nights later it clouds up and a hard rain comes. About nine, the telephone rings three longs and a short. Kid won't answer it; there may be lightning on the line. Finally, Joe picks up the receiver, listens, and motions to the Kid. "This sweet-talkin' little Mescan girl wants you," he says. Kid grabs the phone. He'd risk anything for Beatriz.

He met her in June at an Alpine dance. Later on, he found her fishing at Crescent Lake and helped her catch the limit. They had gotten pretty thick that day. She is Brazilian and rich, and she is spending the summer in Alpine with a Tucson lady who is her aunt and rich. Besides being well-off, Beatriz is sweet and slim, with a sexy walk, husky voice, luminous black eyes, and flawless pale copper skin. She had promised to call.

She tells Kid it's nice to hear his voice and thanks him again for showing her how to catch more fish than anybody else. She and her aunt would love to visit a fire tower. Would the Packard make it to Reno lookout? Kid thinks so and suggests they wait until about Saturday, when the road should be dry again. Joe gets his four days off Friday, and Kid would rather the old boy is not around. Maybe he can sneak Beatriz off for a while. Anyway, he'd sure like to try.

Friday evening, Kid cleans up the tower and mops the cabin before leading the horses and Redeye off to water. Redeye hasn't caused the Kid any problems. Kid has even saddled him up and ridden him around a little, but he's nervous, and that crafty look seems always in his eyes. He's biding his time looking for a chance to do something. Kid doesn't know what. Tommy is due back in a week or so. Maybe that'll cheer him up and settle him down. It'll sure cheer Kid, who's getting his fill of Joe again. Back in the corral, Redeye doesn't eat much and seems a little gaunt, especially compared to Pete, who hasn't been rode at all lately and is so fat he's disgusting.

Kid is just finishing up when he hears the three longs and a short ring from the cabin. He quickly wires the gate latch shut and heads for the phone. It's Owen with orders for tomorrow: "There's no fire danger, so I want you to ride off into Bear Wallow and bring in all the trail signs. They need new paint."

Kid is stunned and disappointed. That's three thousand feet down and six hours riding. It'll kill the day with Beatriz. He can't do any more than just tell her hello then goodbye again. But during the night he has an idea that brings him bolt upright in bed. There's a way to get Beatriz away from her aunt, have her all day to himself, and impress the hell out of her to boot.

By the time Kid hears the Packard next morning, both mounts are fed, ready and waiting in the corral. His saddle sits on Roanie, its stirrups taken up just right for Beatriz. Her legs are nice and long, but still shorter than the Kid's. Old Redeye is a majestic sight there, muscular and grand, with Joe's fancy saddle cinched across his back, ready for Kid to mount. That ought to impress the hell out of any slim, rich, little heiress from Brazil.

Kid winces as the Packard strains up to the cabin. Judging by the sound of it, they've high-centered and busted the muffler. Kid hopes he won't be blamed. After greeting them (Wow! Beatriz is a humdinger in tight levis), Kid crawls under the car. The muffler is nearly dragging. He asks Beatriz to find a piece of wire. "I'll just fix this enough to get you back to Alpine." While she's looking for wire, he tells her aunt his plans for the day, of course leaving out a few key points. He's real sorry the aunt will be left alone so long and hopes it'll be all right.

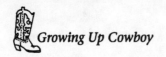

For her part, the aunt is thrilled that Beatriz has such a nice opportunity to see the wilderness. "I just want her to have some fun," she says. "Don't worry about me. I'll climb the tower and play ranger."

The wire Beatriz hands him is for grounding telephones. It's quite heavy. The Kid grunts. "Uh . . . this is kind of hard to twist. Bailin' wire would be better. Where'd you get it?"

"Off the gate," says Beatriz.

Kid swings around until he's looking directly up into the face of Beatriz. From this angle, she's even prettier. "Where?"

"The corral gate. It's no use there; the gate has a nice latch." Her voice is rich and husky. "I can take it back and bring some hay wire."

"No, I'll do it," says the Kid, crawling out from under the Packard. He doesn't run for the corral, not wanting to disturb the two ladies, but he sets a fast trot. When he gets there, the gate is open, and Pete and Roanie are standing head-to-rump, swatting flies off one another.

Redeye is as gone as a fart in the wind.

Kid is lengthening his stirrups again when Beatriz finds him at the corral.

"I've let Tommy's mule run off with Joe's saddle." It's a hard thing to even think about, let alone say. It makes his whole body cold. "I gotta go after him."

Beatriz comes up behind Kid and turns him gently around to face her. She has a hand on each arm. Her face is barely inches away. She is about to say something. Instead, she stares. Even though Tommy and Joe mean nothing to her, Kid knows she sees in his eyes what he feels. She hugs him then; her cheek is smooth and warm against him. "I know you'll catch the mule. And it'll be all right." She drops her hands and turns away.

"I'll find him," he says. Kid doesn't know what else to

say, even though down deep he doubts he'll ever catch Redeye. He's mounted now and heading out. "I guess you'd better go back to Alpine."

"Will you come see me?"

"Yes, once I catch the mule. When you see me, you'll know him and that saddle are back here safe and sound."

Kid is following Redeye's tracks when the Packard crosses the other side of the ridge. Without a muffler its eight cylinders roar like a truck. Kid wishes to heaven his problem could be fixed as easy as a broken muffler.

Redeye has set a good pace. He is holding his head to one side to avoid stepping on bridle reins that leave an unsteady trail in the dirt alongside his tracks. Kid knows they're still in a horse pasture of maybe four square miles. It ends where the drift fence crosses Little Cienega. The mule seems to know this, too, because he's made a beeline for the gate where the trail meets the fence. He sure intends crossing over into the Blue Range allotment to the east, and the enclosure there is big as a county. Kid's best chance of catching him is somewhere along the west of the fence line.

Coming up to the gate, Kid is relieved to see it closed. But he finds his bridle looped over the gate pole, almost as though he'd hung it there. Redeye has hooked it across the post and wedged it off, then turned south following the fence through thickets of aspen and mountain locust. Kid trails him by broken and bent ferns, but he can't ride here because the brush is too thick, so he swings off and leads Roanie. He's getting scratched all over. He looks back; Roanie is bleeding little rivulets here and there, and the leather of Kid's saddle shows new gouges and scratches. Joe's saddle is bound to be getting the same.

It's nearly noon when Kid finally stumbles out of the thickets into a little clearing where two fences meet. Redeye is standing in the corner facing the Kid, his rump against the barbed wire. He doesn't look wild or mean, but

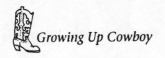

Kid imagines craftiness there in his eyes.

Kid leads Roanie into the clearing and toward Redeye. He's surprised the mule has let himself get cornered this way. He holds out his hand and is moving slowly when Redeye abruptly begins walking toward the Kid. This could be easy. But Redeye's head is high now, his ears have disappeared, and Roanie is holding back on the reins. Redeye is trotting toward the Kid, head high and ears back. Almost too late Kid realizes the mule is charging him, and now there's a hateful, mean glare in the red eyes. Kid whirls and dives aboard a snorting Roanie just as Redeye goes by. Kid is shaking. Charging like a bull, that mule was out to hurt him for sure.

Redeye trots twenty-five yards beyond the Kid and stops. Dust comes swirling up around him as he stands a minute seeming to dare the Kid to come after him. Finally, head high and eyes cold, he turns and follows the west-running fence. He disappears under an old spruce, its branches stabbing at Joe's saddle.

An hour later, a scared Kid not far behind him, Redeye finds a tree lying across the fence and elegantly steps along it. Kid watches in amazement, then dismay, as his prize crosses over into the Blue Range allotment and turns back to the east. There's not another fence for twenty miles. Redeye's got a big portion of Arizona to roam around in now, and he's bound to know it. Kid can only watch, with dread in his heart, as Tommy's beloved mule and Joe's precious saddle disappear to the east.

* * * * *

Early next morning, Kid rides to Double Cienega and meets Owen, who's pulled a trailer with a roping horse up from Alpine. As Owen saddles up, he tells Kid that neither Tommy nor Joe knows what's happened. "Joe's in Springer, and I never had the heart to tell old Tom." Owen doesn't lay into the Kid again today. Goodness knows he'd said enough yesterday, often in words that shouldn't be used on the phone.

Redeye's tracks show at a bog just south of the Cienega where he's come up to drink. Owen's idea is to skirt around the mule, drive him into the open at Double Cienega and rope him there. "If he charged you out of that one corner," says Owen, "we'll never corner him again."

They come upon Redeye just at the edge of the Cienega, and drive him out of thick timber into the open. Redeye takes off across the clearing, which is just what Owen wants. Kid is galloping between Redeye and the trees, and Owen, his horse in a high run, is right behind the mule, shaking out a loop when Redeye suddenly stops, wheels, and heads directly behind the Kid and Roanie. Before Kid can get Roanie turned around, Redeye is back in the trees.

"Stupid-ass donkey knows we can't rope him in those thickets," fumes Owen.

By midafternoon, they've chased Redeye all around the edges of Double Cienega. Owen hasn't thrown a loop, and he's plenty angry. Their horses are worn out, having done a lot more maneuvering and running than Redeye. Now they've lost Redeye, and Owen has had enough. "We'll be back tomorrow with dogs and make that bastard run for a change," he tells Kid.

That night it rains hard. Two bloodhounds can't pick up Redeye's scent until about midafternoon, then they begin to bay off to the southeast. Webb, who brought in the dogs, judges the trail as only lukewarm by the sound of the hounds.

Hitting the trail late in the day that way is the only luck the dogs have left. It gives them a few more hours of life. They bay for a while, the sound moving in a semicircle back toward the Cienega, then fall silent like they've lost the trail. About dusk, Owen, Webb, and the Kid find a tangle of dead dogs at a little pole corral. They've been kicked to death in a narrow loading chute along one side of its fence.

Webb is pretty shook. "I never saw anything like this," he tells Owen. "That killer came in here knowin' he'd draw them hounds right in behind him."

Owen shudders. That evening, he spreads oats in the corral feed trough. "I'll do a little lurin'-in myself," he tells the warden.

Joe comes back to the tower that night. Owen must have told him that the Kid is real cut-up and sorry about losing his saddle because Joe doesn't mention it, though every time he glances toward the Kid, there's a shaming look in his eyes.

The first day, he puts his old saddle on Pete and goes out mule-hunting with Owen. Kid learns later that they jumped the mule off Blue Rim and Owen chased him into the old wild-horse trap under sawed-off mountain. Riding Pete, Joe got so far behind he couldn't help out. Owen tried scaring back the mule and roping shut the gap at the same time, but the mule charged him. "Just like he done to you," he tells the Kid. "I couldn't do a thing but jump on the fence and let him run by."

That evening Pete begins to swell. By dark his legs are as thick as telephone poles. Kid has never seen anything so pitiful, and Joe is carrying on around him. Finally, Owen whispers to Kid, "He's foundered. Take Joe to the cabin and keep him there."

In the cabin, Joe tells Kid, "I'd ought to say goodbye to Pete, but I cain't." Then he begins to cry.

Kid pretends not to notice, even when Joe pulls out a red bandana and wipes his eyes. "Joe, I'm mighty sorry," he says. "I just want you to know that I'm gonna see that you get a new saddle."

"I don't want no new saddle," says Joe, and he raises his voice. "I want my saddle off that goddam mule." He's close to breaking down again when they hear a shot from the corral. A shadow seems to cross Joe's face, but he pulls himself together. He fidgets. He bites off a chew, pats the pockets of his jeans, and takes out a folding knife. Kid hasn't seen it before. It's a beauty with a stained bone handle and chromed springs. He passes it from one hand to the other as though judging its weight. He opens each blade in turn, testing its sharpness against his thumb. "My nephew, he give this to me," he says softly. The Luna Kid has never felt so little and worthless. He's beginning to understand Joe better now.

The oats disappear that night. Judging by the tracks, Redeye came in and helped himself. So, Owen spends the morning taking out the gate and nailing together a pole "trigger" like cowboys use for trapping wild cows in rough country. The poles point in and swing only one way. Once a critter passes through, he can't get out.

Then Owen ties a rope to an aspen at the edge of the clearing and shakes out a slip loop to hang about head high over the trail. "If that trigger spooks him, he'll likely go out this trail at a high trot," says Owen. Kid reasons that Redeye could well choke against the tightening knot if he does run through the loop. Owen is bound to know that.

Owen tells Kid and Joe to check the trap every morning. If they catch Redeye, they're to leave him alone and call Owen, who is needed back in Alpine for now.

Redeye doesn't have a chance to come near Owen's trigger next day. Word has got around. Two cowboys ride up from the Blue, having made a bet they can catch Redeye. They run him all the way to the campground on Beaverhead. He crashes through a tent there and gets away across Black River, jumping right over a campfire and

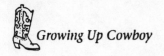

almost knocking a guy into it. Next day Redeye is clearly on his way back to Double Cienega when he comes upon two little girls wading in the creek and charges them with his ears back. They begin screaming. Witnesses say he turned just before running over the kids, but they were nearly scared to death and soaked with water.

Kid wonders. Old Redeye is as spry and strong as any brute ever seen in those parts. He's charged five people now and nobody's got hurt. Why would he run through a campfire unless it was to avoid hitting the fellow standing next to it? He was sure bluffing when he ran up on the kids. But when he charged Kid at the fence corner, it didn't seem like a bluff. It was dead serious, or Redeye ought to be in the movies. And didn't he paw old Tommy?

Having been chased daily by fresh horses for almost a week, Redeye has to be tired to the bone and mighty hungry when he finally pushes through Owen's trigger into the little corral. The tracks next day tell the story. He spent the night eating and resting in the corral, then early in the morning he bit off a cleat holding the trigger shut, went out for water, then came back inside and finished the oats. Leaving again, he spotted Owen's rope and pulled the loose end with either a hoof or his teeth until he'd made a loop big enough to catch an elephant. Then he trotted right on through.

Owen swears like a bee-stung cowboy when he hears.

The day before Tommy gets back to the tower, more cowboys come in to try roping Redeye. They chase him down to the fence above Eagle Creek and lose him there in the brush. Kid hears their report on the telephone to Owen. "That saddle is still on him. We'll make another stab in a day or two."

Owen is not happy about it. "Just stay away from there for a while," he says. "If somebody fools around and runs him through the fence into Eagle Creek, he's gone forever.

Even cows git wild as dragons down in that country."

Kid and Joe are alone at Reno when the ranger brings out Tommy and a horse. Tommy has a bad scar, but it partly disappears in the lines and creases of his face. His cut ear flops more than the other one now, and it has a bad blotch on it. Such a fierce cut and ragged scar might be a detriment to a handsome man but not to a little hump-back like Tommy. Nobody would stare very long at a pimple on a wart.

Kid has missed Tommy but has worried a lot about him coming back. Joe has been poor company. Most of the time now, he toys with his knife and talks endlessly and emptily about his nephew. He still carries a deep-down hurt look about with him. It's his way of punishing Kid for the saddle, and Pete, too. Now, here comes Tommy, whose precious mule is lost, probably forever.

Tommy doesn't offer to shake hands, nor does he speak directly to either of them. He's back to talking to himself. "This ain't my idea of a place to live," he complains at the wall as he shoves his gear under the cot. "I'll hafta watch things here. Some people don't know the difference between what's theirs and what ain't." His voice has the old peevish tones, but the message is clear. It's the same sad Tommy from the first days at Hannigan, only worse now.

Joe speaks up then, addressing the Kid. "It's shore too bad we ain't got a castle to live in, ain't it? With a feather bed and a shit pot for fancy folks."

"I reckon I'll cook my own grub," says Tommy to the wall.

"Some folks jist never was sociable," Joe tells the Kid as loudly as possible. "Maybe it'd be better if they was back in a tent with their bedbugs and mules."

Tommy busies himself with his bedroll. After a while he again talks to the wall. "One feller is lucky Redeye never

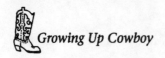

kicked the bullshit out of him, the other that Redeye never sent him flyin' to hell." Kid knows the first is meant for Joe and the second for him.

Suddenly Joe turns on the Kid. It's like Tommy's anger has set him free to let loose some pent-up feelings of his own. "Yeah, you're dilly-damned right," he hisses at Kid. "And some're lucky Owen wouldn't let me do nor say nothin'."

Tommy swings around to face Joe. His voice is squeaky and spiteful. "I heerd tell it was all because of some little half-breed heifer that he done it."

Kid is on his feet and charging for the door while Joe screams hoarsely toward him. "Yeah, by God, I know that's goddam true." His voice cracks and breaks with the release of anger carried deep inside.

While Kid saddles Roanie, a lump in his throat begins to overcome the anger in his heart. He's muttering to himself about "warped and crazy old bastards," knowing full well he's to blame and that there's only one way to save them all now. Redeye can't ever return. Kid kicks Roanie into a gallop past the window of the cabin. Joe is peering out as he goes by.

Holding a high trot, Kid is at Webb's place in Hannigan by noon. Webb listens to the Kid and looks at him sharply. Yes, he'll be glad to loan a .30-30. He understands why it's needed. He's not keen about giving Kid a rope though. "It ain't a good idea, unless you plumb sure know what you're doin'. The mule may drag you down." Then he surveys Roanie. "Well, okay."

On his way to the rim fence, Kid figures the warden knows that Kid is not a good enough roper and that Roanie is too slow to catch Redeye anyway. It doesn't matter—the rope is just to drag the carcass if needed.

Kid strikes Redeye's tracks at a watering hole only a few hundred yards from the fence above Eagle Creek. Kid figures the mule has taken about all the chasing he can stand. He'll be somewhere along the fence, looking for a gap off into rough country below the rim.

Kid is following the tracks when Roanie raises his head and lays back his ears. There's a fairly good view ahead through the trees. Kid can't see anything, but with Roanie acting this way, Redeye can't be far away. Kid gets off, pulls out the .30-30, and levers in a cartridge. Leading Roanie, he walks as quiet as he can toward a little point where he can have a view of the draw and clearings below.

As Kid climbs, an ear comes in sight and a head rises. Redeye has beat him to the point. He's lying there, head up, looking at Roanie and the Kid. Kid stops warily. Redeye rises to his feet and stands there, no more than thirty-five yards away. His eyes are on the Kid. They seem dull and tired and not so red anymore. There's a ragged slash across the still-muscular bulge of his chest. It's partly scabbed over. Blood has run down onto his legs and dried there.

As Kid pulls back the hammer of the .30-30, one ear of the mule flops forward. He seems to recognize the click. Kid plants his left foot ahead and raises the rifle. Redeye lowers his head, as though afraid of falling. Suddenly, what is left of Joe's saddle comes into the gunsights. The saddle is only a skeleton now, its wooden frame bleached ivory. Strings of scruffy leather hang here and there. The horn has broken off. It dangles back toward the seat.

A flush of anger comes over the Kid. The cause of all this anguish stands ready, and this time it'll be easy. If ever a creature deserved killing . . . but he'll get a little closer, maybe draw a charge. It'll be even better and easier if Redeye charges.

Drooping there, Redeye seems somehow no-account, nothing special, just an ordinary mule. He stands as though he is waiting for something. There's no cunning in his eyes now, no fear or anger, only a blank and tired look.

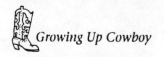

Kid, the animal killer, has never killed one that deserved it until today. Aw, but old Redeye has been brought low, helpless as a baby. Yes, a baby. "Why you poor old bad beat-up baby." Kid holds out his hand toward Redeye. The other ear flops forward. Kid walks closer. "You ol' devil, you think jus' 'cause yore hungry 'n tired, I'm gonna let you off easy, huh?" Kid doesn't know why he isn't afraid of the mule. He's walking right up against Redeye now and has a hand on the ring at the beard, then the cinch buckle. He tugs and pushes. The saddle drops off the other side. Kid pulls at the blanket, which lies nearly crossways on Redeye's back. It's stuck down from saddle sores underneath and stinks horribly. He'll never get it off.

Still talking Tommy's kind of baby talk, Kid puts his rope around Redeye's neck and leads him to the Eagle Creek gate. He drops the gate, removes the rope, and watches Redeye trot off, a corner of the blanket swaying with his limp. That limp isn't nearly so bad as it looked back there on the point. Before disappearing in the trees, Redeye stops and glares back at the Kid. His eyes are bright like the old days. They kind of flash. Kid imagines cunning there. Damn scoundrel. Maybe he was just faking again.

Shit. Would have been quite a prize to lead him in and get credit for roping old Redeye. Sure might have brought a pat on the back from Owen and a dandy-sweet hug from Beatriz, maybe a kiss. She'll be gone. Pete's gone. Redeye's gone. The saddle lies ruined at Kid's feet. Everybody's dues are paid. Nobody came out ahead in this mess. Well, maybe one, but what's a fart in the wind?

At the cabin, Kid smells supper. The door is open as he rides past, and Tommy and Joe are sitting there eating, together. Tommy comes to the door and peers out into the dark. "That you, Kid?" He sounds cheerful.

Kid steps into the cabin carrying the mangled saddle. The lantern casts a circular shadow directly underneath.

He drops it there. "Here's your saddle, Joe," he says.

Then Kid props the .30-30 in the corner. "Redeye's gone," he tells Tommy.

The two old men lean quietly against the table with their own thoughts for a while. Kid sits down to eat.

Finally Joe clears his throat. "Glad you're back, son," he says. "You give us a little scare there."

"Webb, he told us what you was up to," says Tommy, his scar disappearing in a hint of a smile. They hear thunder off to the west. "Good thing you got done ahead of the storm."

Joe moves then to pick up the remains of his saddle. "Jist look at this," he says. "That 'uz sure one tough mule."

"I reckon," says Tommy. "He wrecked a dandy saddle."

The lightning flashes are closer now, brightening shadowy corners of the cabin. A big rain tonight will end the fire season. They'll all be turned off within a few days.

As the first drops patter on the roof, Joe begins to carry on in his old way. "There's only one thing," he says, "that don't wear out or change. That's a diamond. You take the north star, for example. It don't change 'cause it's one helluva big diamond up there in the sky. But my body's been changin' for the worst 'til now it's pretty well done for. Tom's is wore out too, though less than mine. You, Kid, you're wearin' out whether you know it or not. And ain't it a good thing our bodies go downhill jist like our brains, 'cause if they never did, you'd have wore-out brains in a young body. God almighty, think of the trouble that'd cause. Ain't that right, Tom?"

Tommy grins and again the scar disappears. "Well, yeah. It's sure lucky that I ain't able to be nearly as mean as I'd like to be. Heh, heh."

The rain is coming down hard now.

Kid finishes his supper. Nobody speaks as they clean up and bunk down, but just as the lantern light fades into

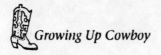

yellow darkness, Tommy sings out, "Hey, Joe."

"Yeah."

"Morenci's lots warmer than Alpine. You wanta winter with me?"

"Well, by jingo, that's a perty fair idee," murmurs Joe sleepily. "I got nothin' to lose."

14

Epilogue

A nd so ends the story, or stories, of Luna Kid, alias the
author. You have learned much about an aspiring
young cowboy who was fairly tested by his environment,
his peers—even himself—and often found wanting. My
editor insists that a few words be added about the meta-
morphic adult who emerged from this bumbling child-
hood, crossed the frontier of the Mogollon Breaks, and
disappeared into the real world.

I must tell you at the outset that except for a few
stresses here and there (brought on, perhaps, by deficien-
cies in the upbringing just described), my adult life has
been quite conventional. However, I've enjoyed some
extraordinary good luck along the way that might be
mildly interesting. So, we shall hurry through the prelimi-
naries to the good part.

A scant year or so after the shotgun conciliation of
Tommy and Joe, I entered military service. After dis-
charge, I went immediately on to college where I obtained

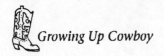

(I didn't say earned) a degree. This was followed by a stint as a high school teacher, which proved to be no less strenuous than branding calves. Finally came marriage, graduate school, a position with a big company, a nice suburban home, four beloved daughters—all bright and beautiful enough to be troublesome at times—winter ski vacations, boating and fishing in summer, etcetera.

I became editor of *The Furrow*, a magazine published by John Deere, the machinery manufacturer. Through sheer good luck (and wasn't Luna Kid due for some?), this happened just at the time my employer entered a period of rapid expansion around the world. Because of *The Furrow*'s success in North America (the *Wall Street Journal* once described it as perhaps the most efficient advertising medium yet devised), overseas managers were demanding editions of their own. To my lot fell the task, if one can call it that, of extending the magazine worldwide. Imagine a traveling salesman flying around the globe offering an exclusive product to recipients who could hardly wait to get it. What can I say? It was a wonderful job.

Of course I learned much from those years of international travel—some of it useful, much of it trivial, some of it startling. I was greatly surprised, for instance, to realize that my isolated homeland in the Mogollon Breaks, including its people, is not altogether an anomaly of the earth. Instead, it is a kind of microcosm. During those busy years, I seldom returned there, but wherever I went, I found reminders of it.

An example is the time in western Spain when companions and I came upon workmen unearthing an ancient Roman town. I was dumbstruck by the setting and scene. Here were Doric columns and an aqueduct sprouting out of a familiar dry gulch near Glenwood, Catron County, USA.

The upper ranch came joltingly out of the past one crisp day, far away from home. All the props were perfectly in place: the oats and potatoes, the black earth and evergreen hills, even the smell of the air and the slant of the sun were just right for those wondrous late September days I remembered. While I photographed the scene, a great deer intruded, as it should. But this was a moose, and this was July on a farm in Norway. Hard to believe I was thirty degrees of latitude and 12,000 miles removed from our little Hell Roaring Ranch, elevation 8,000 feet. I could never imagine a more dramatic demonstration of the effects of altitude.

I'll wager that any homesick South African would cry for joy at first sight of the Mogollon Breaks. Here are the blue hills, the brushy gulches, the canyons, creeks, and bordered flats. For example, stretches of the Limpopo River in Kruger National Park can scarcely be told from lower reaches of a flood-swollen Trout Creek. And the high ridge to the east of this storied river, with its scattering of diverse vegetation, is a dead ringer for Luna Mesa. A dead ringer that is, except for those wild elephants that stared insolently at our vehicle through the acacia trees.

Shades of the malpais caves: I saw something, one day, while traveling through the Peloponnesus of Greece, and asked our driver to stop. Along the country road we examined a place where the bulldozer had cut through a shallow ridge. Here were layer after layer of pottery fragments. I could have filled the trunk of the car in minutes. My Greek hosts were not impressed. As we drove on, I realized why. From top to bottom, every cut along the roadway exposed tons of undegraded rubble from civilizations past. I wondered how in the world they keep these Greek kids in school on nice days.

It seemed that everywhere I traveled I came upon people right out of the Mogollon Breaks. Old T.J., for instance, the shingle-man of Luna, has come to represent in my eyes the one type most numerous among earth's humanity. I have yet to encounter the match for his special personality, yet I saw echoes of him often in all walks of life. He represents for me all the people who work hard and get nowhere. The reasons they fail differ across the board. I think T.J. and many others like him are driven not by ambition but by creativity and curiosity. Pride? T.J. had hardly a milliliter of pride in his cup, but I liked him over Joe, a man whose cup ranneth over with the kind of pride that comes before the proverbial fall.

There are lots of Joes in every country in the world, I've discovered. They are the thousands who strut through life with one question foremost in mind: "What do people think of me?" For them, pride is not a condition of mind and heart to be relied upon always. Rather it is a possession that comes and goes like all other possessions. No wonder such people are unsure of themselves and worry so much. This is not to criticize. Joes are usually good and trustworthy people, and some are very successful in politics and business. But they are stunted in many ways by their pride.

Over the years, I've looked often into the faces of women and seen Dia. And I've looked at the face of womanhood and seen Dia. Dia may have been flat-chested back then (I imagine she still is), but she was not a child; she was a young woman. Likewise, the Kid was a young man. The abrupt ending of that evening with her illustrates, I think, one of the profound truths of the mating game. Women appreciate men and enjoy them. But they tend to be sexually attracted only to a very few men who are very special to them. In a man's arsenal of expectations, the most embarrassing self-deception is when he convinces himself, incorrectly, that some woman lusts for him. Show me the amorous young buck (or old blade) who claims never to have felt the sting of that rejection, and I will show you, as they say in the Mogollon Breaks, a damned liar. Luna Kid may have learned this lesson younger than most, but all men learn it eventually.

Doesn't the sexual revolution change all that? No. Not for the discerning woman who is in touch with her true and natural feelings. It takes a lot more than just wanting to, to succeed with this kind of woman.

When I first met Tommy, I thought he was one of a kind. But as I've traveled the world and through life, I've met his type over and over again. Characterized by bravado, they are the storytellers of the world. They have wonderful memories, they are articulate, they love to quote people, including themselves. Every town of the earth has its Tommy, and it's a lucky thing. Where would we be without them?

Old Cass seemed unique. Like T.J., though, he was just an extreme example of something I've seen in people everywhere but unfortunately not in every person. From Cass I learned to laugh at my ridiculous self, so in that sense, it was he who wrote this book. Cass was a totally ridiculous person, and he knew it; in fact, he reveled in it. Cass tried not to be too dignified ever. If he had a motto, it might have been: "Life will give us plenty of licks that hurt, don't add to it."

A pity of our times is that so many youngsters take themselves so seriously. They view glitches in life as somehow either tragic or romantic, when in fact they're most likely just ridiculous. Cass would have added: "If you can possibly laugh at life, then for goodness sake do that, and don't agonize about it. And don't be afraid to be ridiculous. Everybody else is. Just look around and tune into people. You'll see . . . and laugh."

In my own lifetime I've met approximately fifty people who are in no way ridiculous. Some of them are relatives. Some of them are selfless and very admirable. But none of them is a friend because such people are bearable for only about an hour a year.

Old ridiculous Cass is dead now. T.J., Tommy, Joe,

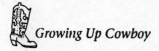

Owen, my father, even Jimmy (who died, much too young, of diabetes) are also in their graves. Many others mentioned here are alive and well. And not a few of them are living yet in the Mogollon Breaks.